CUISINE NATURELLE

Anton Mosimann was born in 1947 at Solothurn, Switzerland. A fourth-generation chef, he first decided to follow the profession at the age of six. He trained and worked in Italy, Canada, Belgium, France and Japan, as well as in his native Switzerland. In 1976, at the age of only twenty-eight, he was appointed Maître-chef des Cuisines at the Dorchester Hotel in London. His skills, energy and innovation brought accolades to the hotel's two restaurants, as well as two stars in the *Guide Michelin*. In 1988 Anton Mosimann left the Dorchester and established Mosimann's, a restaurant-club in Belgravia.

Mosimann is a frequent broadcaster and has made notable television programmes cooking in a council house in Sheffield and contributing as chef to *The BBC Diet*. The successful *Cooking with Mosimann* was his first major television series, broadcast in 1989.

CUISINE NATURELLE

The Way to Better Health, Longer Life and Happiness

Anton Mosimann

PAPERMAC

First published 1985 by Macmillan London Limited

First published in paperback 1987 by
PAPERMAC
a division of Macmillan Publishers Limited
4 Little Essex Street London WC2R 3LF
and Basingstoke

Reprinted 1991

Associated companies in Auckland, Delhi, Dublin, Gaborone,
Hamburg, Harare, Hong Kong, Johannesburg, Kuala Lumpur, Lagos,
Manzini, Melbourne, Mexico City, Nairobi, New York, Singapore
and Tokyo

British Library Cataloguing in Publication Data
Mosimann. Anton
        Cuisine naturelle: the way to better
        health, longer life and happiness.
        1. Cookery (Natural foods)
        I. Title
        641.5′637   TX 741
        ISBN 0-333-37972-1

Designed by Robert Updegraff

Photographs by John Lee

Illustrations by Jane Human

Typeset by Universe Typesetters

Printed in Hong Kong

CONTENTS

ACKNOWLEDGEMENTS

I would like to say thank you particularly to Dr Janet Gale, Lecturer in Health and Social Welfare at the Open University, and also to Lyn Hall (Principal of La Petite Cuisine School of Cooking), Cherry Stevens, Jane Suthering, Sylvia Baumann, Christiane Schröder, Kit Chan, Roy Raiman, Ralph Bürgin, Ian Champion, Michael Bonacini, Clive Howe and to the Kitchen Brigade of The Dorchester.

And a special thank you to Susan Fleming who edited *Cuisine Naturelle*. She is a brilliant editor, and without her help I could not have completed this book.

INTRODUCTION

The pleasures given by a carefully prepared and beautifully presented meal are joyful and unique experiences in themselves. Everyone - old or young, rich or poor - wishes to eat food that is flavourful, original and exciting, however simple that basic food may be. Eating is something that is performed two to three times a day, basically for the purpose of sustaining life, and the preparation for eating merits all the care, love and creativity the cook can lavish upon it.

My philosophies of food and life are the same. They should both be experiences of happiness, serenity and joyful giving. The health of the mind depends on maintaining interest, on being happily and constructively occupied; the physical health of the body depends on controlled exercise, which in turn leads also to alertness of mind. The health of both mind and body are dependent ultimately on how we eat. We are undoubtedly, to a certain extent, composed of what we eat - and excesses of certain foods or basic ingredients can influence physical and mental states and capacities.

Fortunately we can create a balance, whereby good food and good living go hand in hand, a balance that is not in the least difficult to attain. For if moderate amounts of food - the best seasonal vegetables and fruit, the most beautiful of fish, the leanest slices of meat, the least fatty of dairy produce - are prepared with delicacy and eaten with whole-hearted appreciation, we could all be of better temper, more mentally alert, healthier, and could grow with a happiness of spirit, balanced both mentally and physically.

To prepare a meal carefully, with the best ingredients and only the well-being of your guests in mind, is to give them a special gift - not only the gift of a memorable meal, but also the gift of life. In the recipes that follow in this book, I shall show you how to prepare food for life, simply cooked and creatively presented, to encourage good temper, long life and much happiness.

What is Cuisine Naturelle?

In the past, 'good food' and 'food that is good for you' were often seen as mutually exclusive: food could be either one or the other, but never appeared to be both. And yet there is no valid reason why there should be any contradiction between eating well and eating healthily. The basic principles of good cooking – and my own style of cooking – have always been to use the freshest, most perfect ingredients, and to prepare them in the way best suited to them – simply, subtly, to bring out colour, flavour, succulence and goodness. To these principles I have added an extra dimension – the ideas behind Cuisine Naturelle – to create a new unity and balance: the pleasure of enjoying the finest food and cuisine while nurturing the health of the body.

Today, in a Western world newly conscious of the relationship between health and food, people are worried about four main health problems:

○ diseases arising from overweight

○ heart disease and problems of the circulatory system

○ problems of the stomach and digestive system

○ dental problems

The most controllable dietary culprits that are believed to cause or to exacerbate these problems are excessive fats, oils, salt, sugar and calorific intake, as well as insufficient intake of dietary fibre, fresh fruits and vegetables.

Cuisine Naturelle is therefore characterized first by the exclusion of many of these ingredients. In my recipes I use no oil, butter, cream or alcohol, and none of the cooking methods or techniques that require their use. I have also carefully reduced the need for salt and sugar, and as a result of all these exclusions and reductions, the calorific value of many dishes is decreased. By quick and careful choice and preparation of many ingredients - vegetables in particular - dietary fibre and essential nutrients are retained fully for the use of the body.

Exclusions

Butter, oils, cream and alcohol do undoubtedly have their rightful place in good cooking and haute cuisine - contributing to many fine, classic dishes, adding flavour and indeed goodness (for none is essentially *bad*) - but they can have deleterious effects as well. Butter, oils and cream contain fats which increase calorie and cholesterol consumption - both undesirable for the weight- and health-conscious (cholesterol is directly related to artery and thus heart and circulatory problems) - and alcohol not only contains sugar and calories, but can also affect the liver and increase blood pressure.

Where possible, therefore, low-fat equivalents of traditional ingredients have been substituted if necessary - natural yoghurt, fromage blanc and tofu (soya bean curd) instead of cream, for instance - and sauces (often said to be the ultimate test of a chef) are based not on butter, cream or alcohol reductions, but on good stocks of meat, fish or vegetables, or colourful vegetables or fruits. Recipes are given for making many of the above equivalents, but selected commercial varieties, provided that you choose those that contain no colouring, preservatives, etc., could be used instead.

As a result, the visual effect of many dishes is lighter, clearer, with outlines and colours not muted by cream or butter. The natural flavours of many foods, too, are more honest, more *real*, not overpowered by sauces made with alcohol, and the overall experience is thus more carefully focused, defined and enhanced.

Reductions

The exclusion of cream, butter and oils ensures an immediate reduction in the fat content of many foods that already contain fat - even lean meat, for instance, contains some 20 per cent fat. By carefully preparing meat - by cutting away visible fat, and choosing the leanest cuts (as in the following recipes) - a further reduction is obtained.

But Cuisine Naturelle is not designed to be a dogmatic or extreme form of cooking or eating. Some fat in the diet is necessary so that fat-soluble vitamins, such as A, E, K and D, can be absorbed in our bodies. Salt, too, which, in excess, contributes to high blood pressure and strokes, is a mineral needed by the body in small amounts, which vary according to climatic and other conditions. It is required in cookery as well, to set the nutrients in green vegetables, for instance, and, primarily, to season and give flavour. Foods without any salt would not taste so good, but quantities can be reduced, and I have also created some herb mixtures (see page 40) which, when added to a recipe, can reduce the need for salt in that recipe by about 50 per cent.

Sugar too is the 'white death' for many present-day writers on health. It undeniably adds nothing nutritionally to the body except calories, and so my recipes use considerably less. (Artificial sweeteners must never be used, as some can be harmful to health - and taste unpleasant as well.) Many of the recipes that require sugar, the desserts, rely more on the natural sweetness of the major ingredient, normally fruit.

The overall effect of the reductions that characterize Cuisine Naturelle is to reduce calorific intake, and create a new balance of health-promoting ingredients which favour a higher proportion of natural fibre, and lower amounts of potentially harmful ingredients.

The most basic reduction of all, perhaps, is that of quantity of food. Portions are designed not to overwhelm the eater, to look delicate and inviting, to whet and satisfy the appetite, not challenge it to a duel! Hors d'oeuvres are often served as main dishes (which is why that chapter is the longest in the book), accompanied by vegetables and garnishes served on the same plate (sensible as everything keeps considerably warmer and looks absolutely freshly prepared).

Basic Methods of Preparation

The second major characteristic of Cuisine Naturelle must be the methods of preparation themselves. In order to practise the art properly, the cook should not only be enthusiastic, dedicated and continually creative, but must also be aware of the 'scientific' basis of the art - why food acts and reacts in the ways that it does. The cook must understand the structure of food, judge its qualities through the senses of smell and taste, and creatively apply that knowledge to, first of all, the methods of preparation.

Most classical cooking methods can be adapted, with the obvious exceptions of fat-based roasting and deep-fat and shallow frying. Steaming, poaching, grilling and dry sautéing are the basics - all of them quick - for preserving flavour, texture, colour and nutrients, and, above all, the qualities of the foods themselves. Grilling needs no added fat because of the intrinsic fats of meat or fish; sautéing, to seal, sweat or brown ingredients, is done carefully in a dry, non-stick pan, again relying on the hidden fat of meat and the moisture content of vegetables; steaming and poaching are already well known as healthy, controllable methods of preparing food so that their nutrients can be fully taken up and used by the body.

Whichever method is used, it must be done carefully and lovingly, to just the right stage, to retain the valuable properties of the food. Fine cooking must preserve the qualities of fine ingredients.

Ingredients

The basis of fine cuisines all over the world is to be found in the careful selection and correct preparation of excellent ingredients - and the same is, of course, true of Cuisine Naturelle. Choose the freshest seasonal vegetables from the market; the freshest fish (after visiting Billingsgate fish market in London, I cannot wait to return to the kitchen to produce a dish that will do justice to the turbot, lobster or other fish that I have just personally selected); the finest meats or free-range poultry. In fact, throughout the recipes I have tried to avoid the adjective 'fresh'; the foods used in Cuisine Naturelle *are*, and *must be*, fresh.

All canned, processed or factory-produced foods should be avoided. And, although often less easy to obtain, it is undoubtedly true that the best meats are those from animals fed properly, not chemically fattened. Personally, I prefer organically grown vegetables and fruit, and the free-range egg just *tastes* better than that from the battery (unless the chicken has found wild garlic to feed on!).

The raw materials produced by nature are in themselves the finest food, and retaining their original taste is one of the most important principles of Cuisine Naturelle. The good cook should always follow the axiom formulated by the great chef Auguste Escoffier: *'La bonne cuisine est celle où les choses ont le goût de ce qu'elles sont'* (Good cooking is that in which things taste of what they are). It is to that principle above all others - as you will see from the recipes to follow - that I have dedicated my professional life, and this book.

The Presentation

The presentation of any dish, and no less in Cuisine Naturelle, is basic to its enjoyment. The simplest of foods can be placed on the plate to enhance its natural grace, as well as to increase the diner's appetite. For instance, a poached fillet of fish, garnished with a few fresh herbs and colourful vegetables, can please the eye as well as the stomach - for the part played by the senses of sight and smell are probably still undervalued as stimulators of the gastric juices. It is never necessary to have an elaborate presentation.

Sauces, and other garnishes and accompaniments too, add to the visual effect of a dish as well as to its taste (although in general fewer sauces are used in Cuisine Naturelle). A simply grilled chicken breast, arranged on a natural, interestingly seasoned vegetable sauce, is a delight to the eye and ultimately to the palate.

And the plate or dish on which the food is arranged is important too. The best plates upon which to present food are the plainest - the food should be the picture, not the plate. As you will see from the photographs throughout the book, we have used plain black and plain white plates which are a wonderful canvas on which to 'paint' with vivid vegetable and fruit colours.

Menu Planning

This is largely a matter of combining ideas with a large proportion of common sense.

Cooking and eating should be interesting, exciting and different. In fact the art of cooking is just that: no dishes turn out exactly the same twice, and a new sauce or dish may be created by accident. The cook is, in essence, continually an apprentice, constantly sampling, trying again, learning.

Thus a menu should also be interesting, exciting and different. The ingredients for courses should differ in content for interest and nutritional balance - a fish hors d'oeuvre should be followed by a main course of meat or poultry; the textures should excite - no two courses should contain a mousseline, for instance, and crisp vegetables can complement a soft-fleshed fish; the methods of preparation should be varied to create interest - try to avoid two or more courses that are steamed or sautéed.

Colour, too, is a vital ingredient of menu planning, and makes a vital contribution to the finished look and balance of a meal: plan colours carefully, offsetting a poached white chicken breast with a green vegetable and a red garnish rather than a white purée of celeriac, say; and follow with a richly coloured fruit dessert rather than a (white again) milk pudding or ice cream.

Tastes, too, are obviously vital to the success of a dish or a meal - and an imaginative cook is continually experimenting, marrying flavours, to create something new and different (although a good cook, while knowing when to innovate, when to improve, will also know when to leave well alone). Try to include and mix the flavours of sweet, salt, sour and bitter to achieve a good flavour balance: offset the bitterness of Brussels sprouts or chicory with a little reduced apple juice, for instance, to get an ideal medium.

Taste can be like colour. Some people like red, some like blue - neither is right or wrong - and the same applies to taste. Many people just do not *like* a particular taste, or taste combination. An important feature of good menu planning - though often disregarded - is not only to be able to recognize good combinations of tastes, but to remember and respect the tastes of the guests.

Perhaps one of the most important things to remember about menu planning is *not* to plan too meticulously. The good, creative cook should never have set ideas when shopping for the basic ingredients of his or her art - but should buy what is best, what is good that day. You may not have planned to buy melons, but if they look, feel and *smell* good, and seem better than your original choice of fruit, change those plans and adapt. The essential ingredient, in effect, is flexibility.

The Philosophy of Cuisine Naturelle

'Healthy' food does not mean a joyless life of deprivation. On the contrary, I want to celebrate the delights and pleasures of eating food that is light and wholesome and looks irresistible. Cuisine Naturelle is *happy* food, and it was created to ally my basic principles of good cooking to those of good nutrition and health. I was helped enormously in this by two good friends - Dr Janet Gale, who devised and advised on the health and nutrition side, and Lyn Hall, Principal of La Petite Cuisine School of Cooking, whose expertise enlightened the photographic sessions - and I am very grateful to them both.

No longer will it be necessary to pay dearly in terms of health to enjoy good cooking. Cuisine Naturelle has married the two, and I hope that the ideas and recipes on the following pages will bring much happiness to all those who - like me - enjoy living well, eating well and *staying* well.

ANTON MOSIMANN
September 1984

THE BASICS OF CUISINE NATURELLE

By the basics of Cuisine Naturelle are meant the methods of preparation, the methods of cooking - although the words 'to cook' are often misused in the kitchen (there are only a few raw materials that are *cooked*). Anyone who is fully familiar with all these basic methods of preparation - who can understand them, apply them, and use them correctly - can cook anywhere in the world, for they are the multiplication tables of cooking.

Cuisine Naturelle, by its very nature, does not use some methods of basic preparation - those which need oils or butter for success, like roasting or deep-frying, for instance - while many others have been adapted. The following are the major methods of preparation relevant to Cuisine Naturelle.

Blanching
Blanchir

 Blanching means to treat food with boiling water in order to whiten it, preserve its natural colour, loosen the skin or remove a strong flavour or smell. The food can be brought rapidly to the boil in cold water and boiled for a short time, or it can be plunged into boiling water. In both instances, the food must be placed quickly thereafter in cold or iced water to prevent further cooking. Blanching is usually a preliminary to other cooking methods.

Vegetables Place in rapidly boiling, lightly salted water, and bring back to the boil. Drain quickly and plunge into cold water (or cold vegetable stock for added flavour). Remove and use as required. This method guarantees that the chlorophyll-related vitamins and mineral salts are retained in green vegetables. This is also vital before freezing vegetables as it inactivates enzymes and sets the colour.

Blanching also softens marginally - as with salad leaves to be used as a wrapping - and it is useful for removing peel or skin, as with tomatoes. It can also remove the strong flavour of some vegetables - such as peppers, celery, cauliflower or onions - at the same time making some of them more easily digestible.

Potatoes should be placed in deep boiling salted water, and brought to the boil. Remove potatoes quickly and allow to cool on a tray or a towel.

Fruit Blanching in boiling water for a couple of seconds helps remove the skin from peaches, for instance.

Meat and Meat Bones for Stocks These should always be blanched before further preparation. Bring to the boil in cold water. This opens the pores or cells, removing impurities.

Blanching firms up some foods, like sweetbreads, before further preparation. Bring to the boil in cold water before plunging into more cold water.

Chicken Bring to the boil in cold water for white poultry stock. Drain and continue as required.

Blanching Essentials

- A saucepan large enough to hold what you wish to blanch - a whole chicken, or a large quantity of chopped bones.
- Another large container holding cold water into which to plunge the food after blanching.
- Cool the blanched food quickly, using ice perhaps. Food needs to be brought down to below 20°C/68°F as rapidly as possible to prevent bacterial contamination or spoilage.

Poaching
Pocher

Poaching is a gentle and protective method of food preparation which is carried out in a liquid or in a container in a bain-marie at 65-80°C/150 -175°F. Poaching can also be achieved in a double-boiler. The food must be submerged or partially submerged in liquid, and that liquid should barely move. If the temperature of the poaching medium rises above 80°C/175°F, the protein of the food begins to break down.

Poached food, like steamed food, retains flavour, texture and nutrients to a high degree.

Poaching in Liquid Fish above all benefits from the poaching method, in a little liquid or in a court bouillon. Poultry, after being blanched, can be poached in white poultry stock. Offal, too, benefits from poaching, and eggs are, of course, the original poached food (the word poach comes from the French for pocket, meaning the coagulated white surrounding the yolk like a pocket).

Poaching in a Bain-Marie Vegetables, terrines, eggs, custards and desserts can be poached in containers in a bain-marie.

Poaching in a Double-Boiler The same temperature applies to poaching in a double-boiler, or a bowl suspended over quivering water in a pan. This method is used for sauces that require the gentlest of heating.

Poaching Essentials

- A pan large enough for the process is vital - for a whole fish, for instance.
- The poaching liquid - water, stock or court bouillon - must barely quiver: if it bubbles in one part of the pan, it is simmering; if it bubbles all over the pan, it is boiling.
- If poaching in a bain-marie, either on top of or in the oven, make sure the water level cannot reach the top of the individual containers. A roasting tray with small containers, like ramekins, makes an effective bain-marie.
- Many poached foods benefit from being left in the poaching liquid to cool, when they retain their tenderness and juiciness fully.

Simmering

Bouillir lentement

Simmering is the method of preparation between poaching and boiling, when the liquid is at a temperature of between 95-98°C/about 203°F.

Meat For boiled meat, lamb, veal, tongue, start off with lightly salted water or stock, possibly blanching first. Bring to the boil and then allow to simmer. Do not cover.

Clear Broths and Stocks Start off with cold water or stock to extract the flavour, and then simmer. To obtain a clear broth, and to avoid the breakdown of protein, the casserole or pot should never be covered.

Simmering Essentials
○ Any good strong saucepan will be suitable for simmering.
○ The liquid should tremble only, with the slightest movement on the surface.

Boiling

Cuire

To cook food in boiling water or stock to required tenderness - although many so-called boiled foods are boiled only for a short time before being simmered. Meat and poultry would harden if boiled, and fish would break up if boiled throughout the entire cooking time. Boiled beef, for instance, is simmered for the majority of the cooking time after an initial boiling. Boiling can often mean a considerable loss of nutritive value, as many nutrients are thrown away in the cooking liquid.

Boiling is mainly used for pasta, rice and dry vegetables. The working temperature is 100°C/212°F.

Boiling Vegetables Potatoes and root vegetables should be started off in cold water and covered.

Green vegetables should be started off in lightly salted boiling water, in a proportion of one part vegetables to three of water, and preferably left to boil with the lid off - this cooks the vegetables more quickly and retains more vitamins, minerals and colour.

Boiling Pasta Pasta should be started off in hot, slightly salted water and left uncovered, cooking rapidly. Pasta must be cooked *al dente*, in a proportion of 1:10 of water.

Boiling for Reducing Boiling is also used, particularly in Cuisine Naturelle, to reduce liquids rapidly for stocks and sauces. The rapid boiling in an uncovered pan evaporates some of the liquid, thus thickening the consistency and concentrating the flavour.

Boiling Essentials
○ The liquid must be at a rolling boil, with bubbles all over the surface.
○ At all times, follow instructions on whether to cover the pan or not. Never cover pasta, for instance, as it boils over very quickly, and becomes floury.
○ When reducing, salt *after* reduction, not before, as the saltiness can also become concentrated.

Steaming
Cuire à la vapeur

There are three basic methods: the quick steaming of vegetables, meat or fish in direct contact with steam produced by boiling liquid beneath; the prolonged gentle steaming of sweet or savoury puddings, say, where the food does not come in direct contact with the steam; and there is also steaming under pressure as in a pressure cooker. The first is the method most relevant to Cuisine Naturelle: no fat or sauce needs to be added to the food, and fatless food is much easier to digest as well as being much more healthy.

Steaming food over boiling water - or court bouillon or any other aromatic infusion - is more delicate and more controllable than other processes. Instead of rolling around in liquid as in boiling, foods are stationary, thus less likely to over-cook or break up, and are heated gently by the condensation of steam from the boiling liquid. A major advantage is that the water that condenses and drips back dissolves out fewer minerals, vitamins and natural flavours than are lost in boiling. The liquid over which the food has steamed should be used in stocks, soups and sauces.

As steaming is so quick and delicate, it is ideal for fish and shellfish, and for vegetables of all kinds. Meat, poultry, potatoes and rice may also be steamed very successfully.

Steaming Essentials
○ Special steamers are available, but many can be improvised. A large pot with a well-fitting lid (or use foil as well to ensure a good fit) is vital so that there is room for plenty of liquid, thus plenty of steam. A strainer, colander or something like a drum-sieve to fit on to the rim of the pot, or to suspend from the rim, is the next requirement; often a grid or rack that will fit in the pot and that can stand above the water level will be more appropriate.
○ The water must not touch the equipment holding the food. It must boil constantly to produce steam, and it should be watched to avoid boiling dry (have extra stock or boiling water nearby to top up liquid level). The working temperature should be about 200-220°C/400-425°F.

Sautéing
Sauter

Conventionally, foods are sautéed in a little fat; in Cuisine Naturelle no fat is used, and good non-stick pans are vital pieces of equipment. For some foods, like strips of meat, an initial high heat is necessary to seal the outside, in order to retain the juices. The pan must be moved constantly to keep the food moving; or the food itself may be moved with a wooden implement, as in stir-frying. For other foods, like onions or vegetables, a lower temperature is required, so that the substance is 'sweated' and does not brown. Move the food constantly, and maintain the process until it reaches the desired tenderness - still *al dente* with many vegetables, soft and transparent with onions or shallots.

Foods that can be sautéed include onions, vegetables, potatoes, small pieces of meat, poultry or fish; as well as steaks, cutlets, poultry and game breasts, and fish fillets.

Sautéing Essentials

○ The non-stick pans *must* be of very good and heavy quality - cheaper, thinner pans would scorch - and always use wooden or rubber implements so that the non-stick coating is not damaged.

○ Foods to be sautéed should be quite dry, and the pan should not be overcrowded otherwise the food might steam, poach or simmer, not brown.

○ Sautéing needs constant attention, as many foods could brown too quickly and burn, and many could go beyond the desired pink and tender stage (poultry breasts, for example).

○ When sautéing meat, sharply falling temperatures must be avoided otherwise the meat loses too many of its juices and becomes tough.

Grilling
Griller

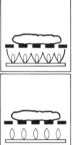

Grilling is a very healthy method of preparation, and can be carried out with either top or bottom open heat. Grilling over charcoal - or over mesquite - lends a particular characteristic taste to the food. A high heat should be used at the beginning to close the pores of the food (between 220-260°C/430-500°F), and then the heat should be lowered (to between 150-210°C/300-410°F), to grill to desired degree of doneness. Use a high heat for smaller, thinner pieces of food, a more moderate heat for large pieces.

Grilling is suitable for small and medium-sized fish, for pieces of meat such as steaks, cutlets, chops and offal, and for poultry, game and vegetables. The process is quick and healthy, most of the fat content dripping into the grill pan beneath. No *added* fat is necessary because of the fat already within many foods to be grilled.

Grill vegetables at a lower heat than meat, as they are smaller in size, and will burn quickly.

Grilling Essentials

○ The grill must be pre-heated to its highest level so that the juices of the food may be sealed in immediately.

○ Follow grilling instructions in individual recipes, as timing is very important.

○ Turn food over with tongs or two spoons (fish with fish slices), as piercing with a fork will allow juices to escape.

Gratinating
Gratiner

A process in which finished dishes are browned or glazed in the oven or under the grill at a high temperature with the heat coming from above (approximately 250-300°C/480-570°F). Often the dishes are covered with a mixture - breadcrumbs, cheese or some other ingredient - which will brown or crisp under the heat. For many uncooked foods with a porous structure, gratinating at a slightly lower temperature can comprise the entire cooking process.

Foods that can be gratinated are soups, fish, meat, poultry, vegetables, potatoes and pasta.

Gratinating Essentials
○ Care must be taken not to *burn* rather than brown the topping or top of the dish.
○ Timing is important, otherwise an already finished dish may be *over*-grilled or over-baked.

Baking in the Oven
Cuire au four

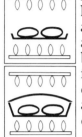

Baking differs from modern roasting only in that food is put into the hot closed oven to bake in a dry heat, *without* added fat. The term is almost synonymous in English with baking bread, cakes and pastries in an oven, but the application is much wider: many other foods can be baked, and the method is particularly suitable for meat, poultry and fish dishes (many of which can be baked in a pastry, foil or other covering), for potatoes, vegetables and pasta dishes, and for pastries and desserts. Foods can be baked in oven-proof and non-stick moulds or dishes, or on non-stick baking sheets, and temperatures range from 140–250°C/285–480°F.

Oven-Baking Essentials
○ The oven temperature stated in the recipe must be followed for complete success, particularly with breads, etc. If unsure of the efficacy of your oven, use an oven thermometer to measure its temperature.
○ Use good quality non-stick ware in which to bake.

Stewing
Etuver

Stewing is the method used to prepare meat, vegetables or fruit in a firmly covered stewing pot or pan, at a lower temperature than boiling. It is in effect much the same as simmering. Without the help of butter or fat, Cuisine Naturelle stewing must start off with an initial quick sautéing (for meat, to sear), or sweating to release juices (as from onions). Liquid such as stock may be added, and the food is covered and stewed at a low temperature of about 110–140°C/230–275°F. As little liquid as possible should be used in most cases, as the stewing process involves steam condensation as well, and so that the gravy or stock may become thick. Depending on the dish, the stock may be served as well.

Stewing is a healthy way of preparation as it retains all the vitamins and minerals of the food within the covered pot. It is particularly suitable for fish, small pieces of meat such as veal, vegetables such as mushrooms, etc., and fruit.

Stewing Essentials
○ A good heavy casserole with a tightly fitting lid is vital.
○ A slow gentle heat must be maintained, whether stewing in or on top of the oven.

STOCKS AND SAUCE BASES

A good rich stock is one of the most important things in fine cooking - for soups, sauces and many other uses - but it is even more important in Cuisine Naturelle where the flavours usually contributed by the excluded ingredients are lacking.

Stocks must be lovingly and carefully prepared. The best and freshest ingredients are vital, the bones should always be cut up small, all fat should be removed, and stock-making should never be hurried. This latter is particularly true of reductions of stock: this process recurs frequently throughout the recipes, as reduced stock takes the place of oils in dressings and other sauces.

Stocks should never be covered, or they will become cloudy. They should be strained carefully - through a fine cloth or sieve - and the liquid should *drip* into the container beneath. Never force the liquid through by pressing the stock ingredients, and the bottom of the cloth or sieve must not touch the strained liquid in the container.

If a stock looks cloudy, it may be clarified in two ways - with the white of an egg or with ice.

To clarify with egg white, mix a lightly beaten egg white with a few ice flakes or cubes and add to the warm stock. Bring to the boil, stirring constantly. The egg white will coagulate, trapping the small particles that cause the cloudiness, and the stock will become noticeably clearer. Strain through a muslin-lined sieve.

To clarify with ice, stir some ice flakes or cubes into the warm stock and bring to the boil, stirring constantly. The coldness of the ice will cause the solid particles to come together. Strain through a muslin-lined sieve.

Also in this chapter are a few of the most fundamental of Cuisine Naturelle sauce bases. These are yoghurt and yoghurt curd cheese, quark and fromage blanc, and they are used throughout the recipes for taste, texture and thickening instead of butter and cream. All are low in fat, and are fairly simple to make at home.

Whether simple or complicated, sauces demand a great deal of care and practice. The new art of cooking presents sauces which are light and delicate, which have their basis in the individual dish itself, and are almost entirely made without flour. Many are made from a simple purée of vegetables, and Cuisine Naturelle sauces are, of course, made without butter or cream, relying instead on reductions of good stocks. Most of the sauces throughout the book are attached directly to the recipe for which they are intended.

Included in this chapter are recipes for filo paste - the one pastry of all the Cuisine Naturelle dishes because it is so light and contains no fat - and a basic recipe for ravioli paste.

Fundamental to the ideas of Cuisine Naturelle is the reduction of salt. The herb mixtures - for fish, meat, poultry and game - will help cut down on salt consumption. They add flavour without overpowering, and by their use can cut the potential salt content of a dish by half.

MEAT BROTH

Bouillon de viande

In order to give the broth a good colour, the onion is browned in its skin.
Dry sauté in a non-stick pan or directly on an electric hot-plate or similar
until brown but not cooked.

Makes 1 litre (1¾ pt)

1kg (2¼ lb)	raw beef bones, chopped and blanched
200g (7 oz)	raw lean beef trimmings
2 litres (3½ pt)	water
50g (2 oz)	bouquet garni (leek, carrots, clove, celeriac and parsley stalks, tied together)
½	browned onion (see above)
	salt and freshly ground pepper

○ Place the soaked and blanched bones and meat in cold water in a saucepan. Bring to the boil and skim.

○ Add the remaining ingredients.

○ Simmer for 2 hours, occasionally skimming and removing the fat.

○ Strain the broth through a cloth or fine sieve, allowing it to drip, and season to taste.

WHITE POULTRY STOCK
Fond blanc de volaille

This white stock is used for poaching chicken, and for white chicken and other sauces. The boiling fowl can be used afterwards for various cold dishes – such as salads, mousses, etc.

Makes 1 litre (1¾ pt)

1	boiling fowl, blanched
2 litres (3½ pt)	water
50g (2 oz)	white bouquet garni (onion, white of leek, celeriac and herbs, tied together)
	salt and freshly ground pepper

○ Put the boiling fowl in a large saucepan, fill up with the cold water, bring to the boil and skim.

○ Add the bouquet garni and seasoning.

○ Leave to simmer gently for 2 hours, occasionally skimming and removing the fat.

○ Strain the stock through a fine cloth or sieve, allowing it to drip, and season to taste.

WHITE VEAL STOCK

Fond blanc de veau

Calves' feet and/or veal trimmings may be used instead of, or as well as,
veal bones.

Makes 1 litre (1¾ pt)

1kg (2¼ lb)	finely chopped raw veal bones, cut into small pieces, and blanched
2 litres (3½ pt)	water
50g (2 oz)	white bouquet garni (onion, white of leek, celeriac and herbs, tied together)
	salt and freshly ground pepper

○ Place the blanched bones in cold water, bring to the boil and skim.

○ Add the bouquet garni and seasoning.

○ Leave to simmer for 2 hours, occasionally skimming and removing the fat.

○ Strain the stock through a cloth or fine sieve, allowing it to drip, and season to taste.

BROWN POULTRY STOCK
Fond brun de volaille

This brown stock is used for brown chicken sauces and the colour and
strength come from the repeated reduction.

Makes 1 litre (1¾ pt)

1kg (2¼ lb)	poultry bones and trimmings, cut into small pieces
50g (2 oz)	mirepoix (carrots, onions, celeriac and herbs)
50g (2 oz)	tomatoes, diced
2 litres (3½ pt)	water
	salt and freshly ground pepper

○ Roast the bones and trimmings in a stew or roasting pan in a moderate oven until brown.

○ Remove the fat with a spoon or strain off. Add the mirepoix and tomatoes and continue to roast carefully for a further 4–5 minutes.

○ Remove from the oven and transfer to a saucepan.

○ First, add 500ml (18 fl. oz) of water, bring to the boil and reduce to a glaze.

○ Add the same amount of water again and reduce to a glaze.

○ Add the remaining water and simmer carefully for 2 hours, occasionally skimming and removing the fat.

○ Strain through a cloth or fine sieve, allowing it to drip, and season to taste.

BROWN VEAL STOCK

Fond brun de veau

Makes 1 litre (1¾ pt)

1kg (2¼ lb)	raw veal bones and trimmings, cut into small pieces
50g (2 oz)	mirepoix (carrots, onions, celeriac, sprigs of rosemary and thyme)
500g (1 lb, 2 oz)	tomatoes, diced
1.5 litres (2½ pt)	white veal stock (see page 24)
1 litre (1¾ pt)	water
	salt and freshly ground pepper

○ Roast the veal bones and trimmings in a roasting pan in a moderate oven until brown.

○ Remove the fat with a spoon or strain off, then add the mirepoix and tomatoes, and roast for another 4–5 minutes.

○ Remove from the oven and transfer to a saucepan.

○ Add half the clear white stock, bring to the boil and reduce by half.

○ Add the remaining stock and reduce to a glaze, about 8–10 minutes.

○ Add the water and simmer for 2 hours, occasionally skimming and removing the fat.

○ Strain through a cloth or fine sieve and season to taste.

LAMB STOCK

Fond d'agneau

Lambs' feet or raw lamb trimmings can also be used with, or instead of, the
lamb bones.

Makes 1 litre (1¾ pt)

1kg (2¼ lb)	raw lamb bones, chopped finely and blanched
2 litres (3½ pt)	water
50g (2 oz)	white bouquet garni (onion, white of leek, celeriac and herbs, tied together)
	some parsley stalks
	salt and freshly ground pepper

○ Put the blanched bones into the cold water, boil up and skim.

○ Add the bouquet garni, parsley stalks and seasoning.

○ Allow to simmer for 1 hour, occasionally removing the fat and skimming.

○ Strain the stock through a fine cloth or sieve, allowing it to drip, and season to taste.

GAME STOCK
Fond de gibier

Any game bird can be used, depending on the recipe for which it is required. By means of repeated reduction, a strong, deeply coloured stock is obtained. Be careful to use only a little salt, as the reduction can and will intensify the natural saltiness of the bones and trimmings.

Makes 1 litre (1¾ pt)

1kg (2¼ lb)	finely chopped raw game bones and trimmings
50g (2 oz)	mirepoix (onion, carrot, celeriac, clove and herbs)
4-5	juniper berries
1 litre (1¾ pt)	brown veal stock (see page 26)
1.5 litres (2½ pt)	water
	salt and freshly ground pepper

○ Roast the bones and trimmings in a stew or roasting pan in a moderate oven until brown.

○ Remove any fat with a spoon or strain off, then add the mirepoix and juniper berries, and continue to roast carefully for a further 4–5 minutes.

○ Remove from the oven and transfer to a saucepan.

○ Add the brown veal stock and reduce to a glaze.

○ Add the water and simmer slowly for 1½ hours, occasionally skimming and removing the fat.

○ Strain through a cloth or fine sieve, allowing it to drip, and season to taste.

MEAT GLAZE

Glace de viande

Similar glazes can be made from fish, poultry and game stocks.

Makes 200ml (7 fl. oz)

5 litres ($8\frac{3}{4}$ pt)   brown veal stock
(see page 26)

○ In your largest pan, simmer the stock until it has reduced considerably.

○ Pour reduced stock into a smaller pan and continue to simmer and reduce.

○ As the stock reduces, keep transferring into smaller saucepans. Keep the edges of the pan clean and clear with a flexible spatula.

○ Simmer until about 200ml (7 fl. oz) remain. Cool and store in the refrigerator. This quantity will be more than adequate for the relevant recipes in this book.

VEGETABLE STOCK
Fond de légumes

This vegetable stock is usually used for soups and vegetarian dishes. It can
be used, reduced, in sauces like tomato, and salad dressings, instead of
olive or other oil.

Makes 1 litre (1¾ pt)

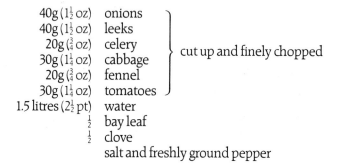

40g (1½ oz)	onions	
40g (1½ oz)	leeks	
20g (¾ oz)	celery	cut up and finely chopped
30g (1¼ oz)	cabbage	
20g (¾ oz)	fennel	
30g (1¼ oz)	tomatoes	
1.5 litres (2½ pt)	water	
½	bay leaf	
½	clove	
	salt and freshly ground pepper	

○ Sweat the onions and leeks in a non-stick pan for 4–5 minutes.

○ Add the remaining vegetables and sweat for a further 10 minutes.

○ Add the water with the bay leaf and clove, and simmer for 20 minutes.

○ Strain through a cloth or fine sieve, allowing it to drip, and season to taste.

FISH STOCK

Fond de poisson

In order to produce a good fish stock, only the bones of the freshest white
fish (sole, whiting or turbot, for instance) should be used.

Makes 1.2 litres (good 2 pt)

1kg (2¼ lb)	broken-up fish bones and trimmings
50g (2 oz)	white mirepoix (onions, white of leek, celeriac and fennel leaves or dill)
30g (1¼ oz)	mushroom trimmings
1.2 litres (2 pt)	water
	salt and freshly ground pepper
	lemon juice

○ Thoroughly wash the fish bones and trimmings.

○ Sweat the mirepoix and the mushroom trimmings in a non-stick pan for 4–5 minutes.

○ Transfer to a saucepan, add the fish bones, trimmings and water, and simmer for 20 minutes, occasionally skimming.

○ Strain through a cloth or fine sieve, allowing it to drip, and season with salt, pepper and lemon juice.

COURT BOUILLON

This stock is used for poaching fish – salmon, turbot, sole – as well as for boiling lobster and shellfish, etc.

Makes 2 litres (3½ pt)

2 litres (3½ pt)	water
200g (7 oz)	carrots, finely cut
100g (4 oz)	white of leek, finely cut
100g (4 oz)	onions, finely chopped
50g (2 oz)	celery, finely cut
1	clove of garlic, unpeeled
5	stalks of parsley
1	small sprig of thyme
½	bay leaf
5	white peppercorns, crushed
3	coriander seeds
	salt
50ml (2 fl. oz)	white wine vinegar

○ Bring the water to the boil.

○ Add all the ingredients and allow to simmer for 10 minutes.

○ Strain through a fine cloth or sieve, allowing it to drip.

FROMAGE BLANC

This basic 'junket' cheese is vital to the principles of Cuisine Naturelle. It is lower in fat than cream cheese – made as below, but with single cream (or at least with full-fat milk) – and can be used in almost all recipes that, before Cuisine Naturelle, would have required the addition of cream.

Makes 1 litre (1¾ pt)

1 litre (1¾ pt)   skimmed milk
¼   junket tablet

○ Place the milk in a very clean saucepan.

○ Using a thermometer, heat the milk to 43°C/110°F.

○ Remove from heat and dissolve the junket tablet in the milk. Stir well and cover.

○ Allow to stand for 24 hours at room temperature until set.

○ Line a colander with cheesecloth and suspend over a large bowl or container (the bottom of the colander must not touch the bottom of the container). Place the set 'junket' in the cheesecloth and let the whey drain out for about 45 minutes.

○ Remove from the cloth and place in a suitable container. It is ready for use immediately, but can be kept in the refrigerator for up to 2 days.

QUARK
Simple curd cheese

Makes about 300ml ($\frac{1}{2}$ pt)

1 litre ($1\frac{3}{4}$ pt)   skimmed milk
juice of $\frac{1}{2}$ lemon

○ Bring the milk just to the boil, then add the lemon juice.

○ Remove pan from the heat, and leave to settle for a while.

○ Bring to the boil again, then let the milk cool once more. It will have curdled.

○ Line a colander with cheesecloth or muslin and place over a deep pan or bowl (so that the colander is suspended and does not touch the bottom of the container).

○ Place the curdled milk in the cheesecloth and let the whey drain away.

○ Take the corners of the cheesecloth and tie tightly with string, and hang up over the container to ensure that the whey drains away completely.

○ This takes approximately 1 hour. Don't press the cloth as this affects the flavour, and the quark will become sticky.

○ Take the quark out of the cheesecloth and put in the refrigerator to cool before use.

HOME-MADE YOGHURT

Yogourt maison

Yoghurt may be made in the following way, or in a commercial yoghurt-maker. Skimmed milk should be used in Cuisine Naturelle, as well as low-fat natural yoghurt.
Keep a little yoghurt as a starter for the next batch, but every few weeks use the commercial live variety which will have the right balance of culture. You can also make yoghurt in the same way from goat's milk.

Makes about 750ml (1¼ pt)

1 litre (1¾ pt)   skimmed milk
15ml (1 tbsp)   low-fat natural yoghurt

○ Bring the milk to the boil.

○ Cool to blood heat – 37°C/98.6°F.

○ Put the yoghurt into a wide-necked jar, pour the cooled milk over it, and whisk vigorously.

○ Cover the jar and put in a warm place overnight, or for a minimum of 6 hours, by which time it will have thickened into a delicious natural yoghurt.

○ Cool in the refrigerator for a few hours before use.

○ Yoghurt should never be over-heated in cooking or it might curdle.

YOGHURT CURD CHEESE

Curd cheese made from freshly made natural yoghurt is very similar to quark,
and can be used in any recipe that specifies either curd cheese or quark.
You can also make a curd cheese from freshly made goat's-milk yoghurt.

Makes about 500ml (18 fl. oz)

750ml ($1\frac{1}{4}$ pt)   freshly made,
low-fat natural yoghurt

○ Line a sieve or colander with cheesecloth or muslin, and suspend over a deep bowl.

○ Put the yoghurt into the sieve, cover, and leave for about 6 hours, or until all the whey has drained away.

○ Cool and use as soon as possible.

TOMATO CONCASSE

Tomates concassées

One of the basic sauces used in Cuisine Naturelle. It has very few calories, is very light and colourful, and has a good flavour which goes well with both fish and meat.

4 PEOPLE

1kg (2¼ lb)	ripe tomatoes
20g (¾ oz)	shallot, finely chopped
1	whole clove of garlic, unpeeled
	a few sprigs of oregano and thyme
	salt and freshly ground pepper

○ Remove the stalks from the tomatoes and then blanch in hot water for approximately 12 seconds. Plunge into iced water and then peel.

○ Cut the peeled tomatoes in half, remove and discard the seeds, and chop into small pieces.

○ Sweat the shallot and whole clove of garlic well, without colouring, in a large non-stick pan.

○ Add the tomatoes and herbs and season with salt and pepper.

○ Cover and cook carefully for about 15 minutes until soft and all the liquid is evaporated.

○ Remove the garlic clove and herbs and, if necessary, season again with salt and pepper.

FILO PASTE

This pastry – the only one used in Cuisine Naturelle recipes – is here made without oil or butter. It must be rolled extremely thin, and when baked is crisp and light.

Makes 650g (1¼–1½ lb)

300g (11 oz)	strong white bread flour
100g (4 oz)	cornflour
2.5ml (½ tsp)	salt
250ml (9 fl. oz)	water

○ Sieve the flour, cornflour and salt together into a bowl. Make a well in the centre.

○ Put about half the water into the well, and gradually draw the flour into the water, mixing smoothly and evenly. Add the remaining water and mix until the dough is smooth and does not stick to the hands.

○ Cover the dough with a damp cloth and leave to rest for 1–2 hours in a cool place. This allows it to develop its elasticity fully.

○ Cut the dough into quarters, and cover the pieces not being rolled with a damp cloth. Start rolling one piece out, gradually making the sheet thinner and thinner. Use plenty of flour, and it helps to warm the dough to make it pliable – cover with an inverted hot aluminium bowl.

○ If the dough sheet becomes too large and unwieldy, cut in half and continue to roll. When as thin as possible by rolling, place the sheet over the back of the hand, and pull gently down from the edges to stretch even more. Work carefully so that it does not break.

○ Roll other pieces of dough in the same way, and cover dough and sheets at all times with a damp cloth. Use sheets as quickly as possible.

RAVIOLI PASTE

Pâte à ravioli

This paste can also be used as the basis for Chinese-type dumplings – for soup, etc., and for tortellini.

4 PEOPLE

100g (4 oz)	flour, sieved
25g (1 oz)	semolina
$\frac{1}{2}$	egg
	pinch of salt
50ml (2 fl. oz)	water

○ Mix the flour and semolina together, then make a well in the centre.

○ Place the half egg, salt and water in the well.

○ Gradually mix the flour in towards the middle.

○ Knead the mixture to a smooth firm paste, then leave to rest for 1–2 hours before use.

HERB MIXTURES
Mélanges des herbes

The blending of herbs warms the spirit and delights the sense of taste and smell. Their flavour should never dominate a dish or product, but should create a harmony.
These herb mixtures have been created to cut down on the use of salt. The proportions have been very carefully worked out so that the flavours of the herbs do not overpower the dish in which they are used.

For fish and shellfish

10ml (2 tsp)	dill, finely cut
5ml (1 tsp)	thyme, finely chopped
5ml (1 tsp)	basil, finely cut
5ml (1 tsp)	chervil, plucked apart with the fingers
2.5ml ($\frac{1}{2}$ tsp)	fresh coriander, leaves pulled off stalks, and plucked apart with the fingers
2.5ml ($\frac{1}{2}$ tsp)	tarragon, finely snipped with scissors

For meat and poultry

10ml (2 tsp)	thyme	
7.5ml (1$\frac{1}{2}$ tsp)	marjoram	finely chopped
5ml (1 tsp)	rosemary	
2.5ml ($\frac{1}{2}$ tsp)	oregano	
5ml (1 tsp)	basil	finely cut
1.25ml ($\frac{1}{4}$ tsp)	sage	

For game

10ml (2 tsp)	rosemary	
5ml (1 tsp)	savory	finely chopped
5ml (1 tsp)	thyme	
2.5ml ($\frac{1}{2}$ tsp)	juniper berries, crushed	
2.5ml ($\frac{1}{2}$ tsp)	tarragon, finely snipped with scissors	

For vegetables

5ml (1 tsp)	oregano, finely chopped
5ml (1 tsp)	dill, finely cut
5ml (1 tsp)	chervil, plucked apart with fingers
5ml (1 tsp)	borage, finely cut

○ Use only fresh herbs, cut, snip and chop as specified, and mix all together. Use a pinch or as much as liked in individual recipes, and you will find that the need for salt is reduced by at least 50 per cent.

○ Fresh herbs are best, of course, but the mixtures can be made up and kept in the freezer in small yoghurt pots.

○ Chopped garlic can be added to the mixtures if liked, but in small quantity only as it can be overpowering (and it should never be frozen).

HORS D'OEUVRES

Hors d'oeuvre means, literally, 'apart from the main work', and thus is the prelude to the high point of a meal, usually a main course of meat or fish. Served before the meat, as an appetizer for what is to come, the hors d'oeuvre should, however, offer a clear contrast to the succeeding courses. As it is meant to excite the palate, but not appease hunger, it must be light; as it is the introduction to the meal, it should be interesting in conception as well as exciting for the eye - for beauty of ingredients, colour, and arrangement on the plate are all major contributors to the enjoyment of a dish or meal.

The recipes in this section have been designed especially to fulfil all the foregoing, as well as follow the basics of Cuisine Naturelle. It is commonly acknowledged these days that people are eating considerably less - which is desirable for good health - and none of the following recipes contains the ingredients that are excluded from Cuisine Naturelle - butter, oils, cream or alcohol. Many of the hors d'oeuvres could be eaten as a light main course, or expanded to serve as a main course; indeed two hors d'oeuvres could be served *instead* of a main course. Thus this section is the longest in the book.

The majority of recipes consist of a colourful, decorative and healthful salad base with a little added meat or fish protein - the ideal prelude to a lighter meal. Here also are thin slices of meat or fish to excite the palate, vegetable and fish terrines, as well as many ideas for light and attractive pasta hors d'oeuvres.

To cut down on salt, one of the herb mixtures (see page 40) could be used instead of some salt in any of the recipes.

CRAB SALAD WITH COCONUT

Salade de crabe à ma façon

For a perfect presentation, saw two coconuts in half and saw off a slice at
the bottom of each half so that it will stand properly.

4 PEOPLE

225g (8 oz)	white crab meat
15ml (1 tbsp)	finely chopped shallots
1	tomato, skinned, seeded and cut into thin julienne strips
1	stick of celery, trimmed and cut into thin julienne strips
50g (2 oz)	fine green beans, trimmed and blanched
25g (1 oz)	shredded fresh coconut
	juice of $\frac{1}{2}$ lemon
15ml (1 tbsp)	red wine vinegar
1	lettuce heart
1	head of radicchio
2	heads of chicory
2	pink grapefruit
1	orange
	salt and freshly ground pepper
15ml (1 tbsp)	freshly cut chives

○ Mix together the crab meat, shallots, tomato and celery julienne, green beans and coconut.

○ Moisten with lemon juice and vinegar, and season to taste with salt and pepper.

○ Wash and dry the salad leaves.

○ Cut away the peel and white pith from the grapefruit and orange and carefully remove all the separate segments of fruit.

○ Arrange the salad leaves in four halved coconut shells (or on plates).

○ Spoon the crab mixture on top and garnish with the grapefruit and orange segments. Sprinkle with chives and serve at once.

SQUID SALAD
WITH MUSTARD AND HERB DRESSING
Salade de calamares à la sauce moutarde et aux herbes

4 PEOPLE

6	squid, about 12cm (4½ in) body length
	juice of ½ lemon
2	heads of chicory, cut into leaves, washed and dried
1	small head of lettuce, prepared, washed and dried
1	medium tomato, peeled, seeded and cut into strips
	salt and freshly ground pepper

Mustard and herb dressing

50g (2 oz)	quark (see page 34)
20ml (4 tsp)	tarragon vinegar
10ml (2 tsp)	soya sauce
5ml (1 tsp)	herb mustard
10ml (2 tsp)	cut fresh herbs (such as chervil, chives, parsley, basil)
30ml (2 tbsp)	vegetable stock (see page 30)
	salt and freshly ground pepper

○ Take the squid by the tentacles, pull off the heads, and remove the insides and spines.

○ Cut off the tentacles below the eyes and put to one side.

○ Loosen the gristle from inside the squid and pull out.

○ Remove the ink sacs and any fluid. (Save the ink for making black noodles or squid sauce.)

○ Wash the body and tentacles well and place on kitchen-paper towels.

○ Chop the tentacles, and peel the outer skin from the body.

○ Slice the meat into small pieces. Season with salt, pepper and lemon juice.

○ For the dressing, mix all the ingredients together in a liquidizer, or with a whisk, and season to taste with salt and pepper.

○ Sauté the squid very quickly in a non-stick pan until opaque.

○ Put some mustard and herb dressing on a plate, and place the sautéed squid pieces on top. Toss the salad ingredients in a little dressing and arrange on the side of the plate.

WHITE AND GREEN ASPARAGUS SALAD WITH SCALLOPS

Méli-mélo d'asperges et coquilles St-Jacques

4 PEOPLE

6	medium white asparagus tips, peeled
16	small green asparagus tips, peeled
12	large fresh scallops
1	new carrot, peeled
60ml (4 tbsp)	low-fat natural yoghurt
	juice of $\frac{1}{2}$ lemon
1	heart of Cos lettuce, washed and dried
1	heart of oak leaf lettuce, washed and dried
	a few leaves of curly endive
	salt and freshly ground pepper
	fresh chervil to garnish

○ Cook the asparagus tips in salted water for 2–3 minutes until just tender. Drain, then cool quickly in ice-cold water. Drain again and keep on a damp cloth. Cut white asparagus in half lengthways.

○ Open the scallops, using the tip of a small, sharp knife to ease the scallop apart. Scoop from the shell with a soup spoon. Remove and discard the brown frill surrounding the white flesh and the coral. Wash well, then cut the white parts in half.

○ Make channels down the length of the carrot with a cannelle knife, then slice the carrot thinly. Blanch slices in boiling water for 1 minute. Drain, then cool in iced water. Drain.

○ Mix together the yoghurt and lemon juice. Season with salt and pepper.

○ Arrange the salad leaves, asparagus and carrots on individual plates. Spoon a little yoghurt on to each plate.

○ Sauté the coral quickly in a non-stick pan for 15 seconds. Add the scallops and sauté for a further 15 seconds. Season to taste with salt and pepper, and arrange on top of the salad.

○ Garnish with tiny sprigs of chervil.

SPINACH SALAD WITH STILTON SAUCE

Feuilles d'épinards en salade au Stilton

Fresh raw spinach is delicious, but tender lettuce, endive, or radicchio may
be used instead.

4 PEOPLE

1	red pepper
250g (9 oz)	tender spinach leaves, thick stalks removed
75g (3 oz)	bread
1	clove of garlic, skinned and crushed
10ml (2 tsp)	lemon juice
5ml (1 tsp)	strong mustard
200g (7 oz)	low-fat natural yoghurt
40g ($1\frac{1}{2}$ oz)	Stilton cheese
15g ($\frac{1}{2}$ oz)	parsley, chopped
5g ($\frac{1}{4}$ oz)	basil, cut
	salt and freshly ground pepper

○ Bake the pepper in the oven at a high temperature, turning occasionally, until dark spots appear on the skin.

○ Remove from the oven and cover for 3–4 minutes with a damp cloth. Remove the skin, cut pepper in half, take out the core and seeds, and cut the flesh into fine strips.

○ Wash the spinach well, drain and dry well on a towel.

○ Cut the bread into small cubes, and bake in the oven at 200°C/400°F/Gas 6 for about 10 minutes until golden. Add the crushed garlic, and mix well to flavour all the cubes.

○ Mix the lemon juice, mustard and yoghurt together well. Crush the Stilton with a fork and mix into the yoghurt. Season to taste.

○ Put the spinach leaves and red pepper strips into a bowl. Pour the sauce over them and mix in well.

○ Sprinkle with parsley, basil and garlic croûtons. Serve immediately, otherwise the tender spinach will quickly fall apart.

CURLY ENDIVE WITH SMOKED HAM AND WALNUT SALAD

Salade d'endive au jambon fumé et aux noix

4 PEOPLE

100g (4 oz)	shelled walnuts
100g (4 oz)	lean smoked ham, cut into thin strips
1	small iceberg lettuce
½	head of curly endive
100g (4 oz)	red onion, cut in fine rings, or spring onions, sliced
7.5ml (1½ tsp)	honey
50ml (2 fl. oz)	wine vinegar
	salt and freshly ground pepper

○ Place the walnuts on a baking tray in the oven at 180°C/350°F/Gas 4 for about 10 minutes until golden. Allow to cool slightly, then rub off as much skin as possible. Roughly chop the nuts.

○ Sauté the ham in a non-stick pan until crisp. Remove from the pan and reserve any meat juices in the pan.

○ Wash and dry the lettuce and curly endive and tear into bite-sized pieces. Place in a large bowl with the nuts, ham and sliced onion.

○ Add the honey to the pan and heat until dissolved. Add the vinegar and bring to the boil. Pour immediately over the salad and toss well.

○ Season with salt and pepper and serve at once.

White and Green Asparagus Salad with Scallops (see page 46)

Stuffed Courgette Flowers with Red Pepper Sauce (see page 91)

RAW MUSHROOM SALAD

Salade de champignons crus

Mushrooms are a perfect Cuisine Naturelle vegetable, containing no sugar
or starch. Here, served raw, they retain their full nutritional value.

4 PEOPLE

100ml (4 fl. oz)	buttermilk
	or freshly soured skimmed milk
100g (4 oz)	fromage blanc (see page 33)
15ml (1 tbsp)	lemon juice
1	small onion,
	skinned and finely chopped
30ml (2 tbsp)	freshly chopped parsley
225g (8 oz)	button mushrooms, washed and trimmed
1	lettuce heart, washed and dried
1	tomato, cut into 8 wedges
15ml (1 tbsp)	freshly cut chives
	pinch of salt and freshly ground pepper

○ Mix together the buttermilk, fromage blanc, lemon juice, onion and parsley until as smooth as possible. Season to taste with a little salt and pepper.

○ Thinly slice the mushrooms and carefully mix into the sauce. Cover and leave to marinate for 30 minutes.

○ Mix well to coat the mushroom slices evenly, then drain.

○ Arrange the lettuce leaves and mushroom salad on each of four plates. Garnish with the tomato wedges and chives.

NETTLE SALAD
WITH GREEN TOMATOES AND SORREL

Salade d'orties aux tomates vertes et oseille

Gather the nettle leaves (and tops too) with gloves. As sorrel contains oxalic acid, only one leaf per person is used, but its sour and refreshing taste is a delicious addition to any salad. To vary the recipe, 100g (4 oz) finely sliced Parma ham can be mixed with the sauce and added to the salad.

4 PEOPLE

100g (4 oz)	tender young nettle leaves
50g (2 oz)	dandelion leaves
	a few dandelion flowers
4	sorrel leaves

Dressing

90ml (6 tbsp)	strong vegetable stock (see page 30)
45ml (3 tbsp)	wine vinegar
4	green tomatoes, skinned, seeded and diced
	salt and freshly ground pepper

○ Wash the nettles, dandelion leaves and flowers, and the sorrel.

○ Finely shred the sorrel and mix together with the nettles and dandelions.

○ For the dressing, whisk together the stock, vinegar, salt and pepper. Add the tomatoes.

○ Warm the dressing gently in a basin over a pan of simmering water.

○ Pour the dressing over the salad, mix carefully and serve immediately.

SALAD WITH RUNNER BEANS
AND SWEETBREADS

Mélange de salades aux ris de veau

4 PEOPLE

250g (9 oz)	calf's sweetbreads
1	onion, chopped
1	carrot, chopped
1	leek, chopped
1	stick of celery, chopped
10	black peppercorns, crushed
3	juniper berries
1	bay leaf
150g (5 oz)	runner beans
60ml (4 tbsp)	reduced white veal stock (see page 24)
30ml (2 tbsp)	wine vinegar
2	small shallots, finely chopped
$\frac{1}{2}$	head of curly endive
$\frac{1}{2}$	head of oak leaf lettuce
$\frac{1}{2}$	bunch of watercress
2	medium-sized tomatoes, seeded and diced
	a few sprigs of flat leaf parsley, cut into julienne
	salt and freshly ground pepper

○ Wash the sweetbreads, then leave to soak for 2 hours, changing the water frequently.

○ Cook in lightly salted water with the onion, carrot, leek, celery, peppercorns, juniper berries and bay leaf for about 30 minutes until tender. Drain and remove skin from sweetbreads. Discard vegetables.

○ Trim and cut the runner beans diagonally into 2.5cm (1 in) lengths. Blanch in boiling salted water for about 1 minute. Refresh in ice-cold water. Drain.

○ Make a dressing with the reduced stock, vinegar, shallots and seasoning.

○ Slice the sweetbreads and marinate in half the dressing for about 8–10 minutes. Wash the salad leaves and toss in remaining dressing.

○ Arrange salad leaves and beans on four individual plates, and place the sweetbreads on top.

○ Garnish with tomato dice and julienne of parsley.

QUAIL AND ARTICHOKE SALAD WITH NUTS

Salade d'artichauts et cailles aux noix

4 PEOPLE

4	globe artichokes
60ml (4 tbsp)	strong vegetable stock (see page 30)
30ml (2 tbsp)	wine vinegar
4	quails
1	head of oak leaf lettuce, washed and dried
4	pieces of lamb's lettuce, washed and dried
4	walnut halves, skinned and chopped
	salt and freshly ground pepper

Sauce

25g (1 oz)	*each* of onion, leek and carrot, diced
3	juniper berries
1	sprig of thyme
$\frac{1}{4}$	bay leaf
1	tomato, diced
425ml ($\frac{3}{4}$ pt)	water

○ Break off the stalks of the artichokes close to the base. Wash artichokes well, then cook in boiling salted water with a dash of vinegar or lemon juice. Cool, remove the leaves and choke and trim the hearts.

○ Mix the stock and vinegar together with salt and pepper to taste.

○ Cut the artichoke hearts into thin slices and marinate in about half this dressing.

○ Remove the breasts from the quails and reserve the legs and carcass for the sauce.

○ To make the sauce, sauté the quail trimmings in a non-stick pan until well browned on all sides. Add the vegetables and herbs, and continue to sauté for a few minutes. Add water and simmer for about 30 minutes.

○ Strain sauce through a fine cloth and return to a clean pan. Bring to the boil and boil until reduced by half.

○ Sauté the quail breasts in a non-stick pan for 1 minute on each side, or until they are still just pink.

○ Arrange the salad leaves, artichoke slices and walnuts on the individual plates. Spoon over the dressing.

○ Arrange the quail breasts on top and glaze with sauce. Serve at once.

WARM CHICKEN LIVER SALAD WITH YOGHURT DRESSING

Salade de foie de volaille tiède, sauce au yogourt

The fresh yeast makes this dressing light and foamy, and gives it a pleasant, nutty flavour.

4 PEOPLE

225g (8 oz)	dandelion leaves or 1 curly endive, well washed and torn
4	tomatoes, skinned and seeded
200g (7 oz)	chicken livers, trimmed, large ones cut in half
30ml (2 tbsp)	freshly cut chives
	salt and freshly ground pepper

Yoghurt dressing

100g (4 oz)	low-fat natural yoghurt
10ml (2 tsp)	wine vinegar
10ml (2 tsp)	soya sauce
5ml (1 tsp)	fresh yeast
10ml (2 tsp)	cut mixed fresh herbs (such as parsley, dill, basil)
10ml (2 tsp)	finely chopped onion
1	sliver of garlic, crushed
2.5ml (½ tsp)	English mustard
	salt and freshly ground pepper

○ Arrange the salad leaves on four individual plates.

○ Cut the tomatoes into julienne strips.

○ Season the chicken livers and sauté in a non-stick pan until lightly browned on all sides, but still pink in the centre.

○ Arrange livers on the salad leaves, and sprinkle with tomato julienne and chives.

○ For the dressing, mix all the ingredients together until evenly blended, and season to taste.

○ Serve the salad at once, with the yoghurt dressing passed separately.

COTTAGE GARDEN SALAD
Salade du jardin

A basic – and delicious – salad, which can be served as an hors d'oeuvre or
an accompanying salad to a main dish.

4 PEOPLE

1	small lettuce
1	small head of radicchio
100g (4 oz)	spinach leaves, tough stalks removed
1	bunch of watercress, stalks removed
100g (4 oz)	raw mushrooms, thinly sliced
75g (3 oz)	carrots, peeled and thinly sliced
50g (2 oz)	radishes, thinly sliced
15ml (1 tbsp)	chives, finely cut

Dressing

100g (4 oz)	red pepper, cored, seeded and chopped
150ml ($\frac{1}{4}$ pt)	skimmed milk
25g (1 oz)	onion, chopped
1	medium tomato, peeled and finely chopped
5ml (1 tsp)	French mustard
	a pinch of paprika
	salt and freshly ground pepper

○ Wash and dry the salad and spinach leaves. Tear into bite-sized pieces, and mix with the washed watercress leaves.

○ Combine the mushroom, carrot and radish slices with the salad leaves. Sprinkle with chives.

○ For the dressing, steam the red pepper pieces for 3–4 minutes until just tender. Cool, then purée with the remaining ingredients in a liquidizer until well mixed. Season to taste with salt and pepper.

○ Mix dressing into the salad leaves just before serving.

THIN SLICES OF HALIBUT WITH VEGETABLES

Eminçé de flétan oriental

As the halibut is to be eaten simply marinated, it must be of top quality and
very fresh.

4 PEOPLE

450g (1 lb)	fillet of halibut, skinned
	juice of 1 lemon
30ml (2 tbsp)	Meaux mustard
30ml (2 tbsp)	Dijon mustard
30ml (2 tbsp)	rice vinegar
60ml (4 tbsp)	fish stock (see page 31)
50g (2 oz)	Daikon (white radish) ⎫
50g (2 oz)	red radish ⎪
50g (2 oz)	carrot ⎬ cut into julienne strips
25g (1 oz)	celery ⎭
25g (1 oz)	enoki mushrooms
15g ($\frac{1}{2}$ oz)	flaked almonds, toasted
4	small bunches of lamb's lettuce
	salt and freshly ground pepper

○ Slice the halibut very thinly, and season with lemon juice, salt and pepper.

○ Leave to marinate for 5–10 minutes in a cool place.

○ Meanwhile mix the two mustards, vinegar and fish stock together. Season well and
leave to stand at room temperature. Mix again before serving.

○ Spoon the mustard sauce over the fish.

○ Garnish with the julienne of vegetables, mushrooms, flaked almonds and lamb's
lettuce.

MARINATED SCOTTISH SALMON

Saumon d'Ecosse mariné

Here are two methods of 'pickling' salmon: one which takes 24 hours, and one which takes only 10–15 minutes. As the salmon in both cases is to be served virtually raw, it must be extremely fresh. In the first recipe, the quantity of sugar has been reduced to a minimum.

Version 1   ABOUT 10 PEOPLE

1.5kg (3–3½ lb)	whole Scottish salmon
30g (1¼ oz)	salt
20g (¾ oz)	sugar
25g (1 oz)	fresh dill
15ml (1 tbsp)	white peppercorns, coarsely ground

○ Carefully fillet the salmon and remove the bones.

○ Coat with a mixture of the remaining ingredients, place in a suitable dish, cover and store in the refrigerator.

○ Marinate the fish for 24 hours, occasionally moistening it with the liquid that is produced.

○ Remove from the marinade and cut as smoked salmon. Use the dill as garnish.

Version 2   4 PEOPLE

400g (14 oz)	fresh fillet of salmon, (after skinning and trimming well)
	juice of 2 limes
15g (1 tbsp)	*each* of freshly cut chives, chervil and finely snipped tarragon
15ml (1 tbsp)	Meaux mustard
	salt and freshly ground pepper
2	small lemons to garnish

○ Cut the salmon into very thin slices and arrange on a suitable dish.

○ Whisk together the remaining ingredients and pour over the salmon. Leave to marinate for 10 minutes.

○ Garnish simply with lemon halves. If serving as a main course, an ideal accompaniment is the Raw Mushroom Salad (see page 49).

Marinated Scottish Salmon with Poached Eggs (see page 57)

Quail and Artichoke Salad with Nuts (see page 52)

Grilled Seafood Sausage with Carrot Leaf Sauce (see pages 114-15)

Potted Scottish Salmon Terrine with Vegetables (see page 58)

MARINATED SCOTTISH SALMON WITH POACHED EGGS

Saumon d'Ecosse mariné aux oeufs pochés

The first method is more suitable for this dish. The sauce is not vital,
but it adds a piquant flavour.

4 PEOPLE

4	eggs, size 3
	water for poaching,
	with a spot of vinegar added
12	thin slices of marinated salmon
8	lettuce leaves, well washed and dried
10ml (2 tsp)	lemon juice
	salt, freshly ground pepper, and paprika
	a little dill for garnish

Sauce

150ml ($\frac{1}{4}$ pt)	fromage blanc (see page 33)
20g ($\frac{3}{4}$ oz)	French mustard
30ml (2 tbsp)	liquid from the marinade, strained
	Cayenne, salt and freshly ground pepper
	a little fresh dill

○ Poach the eggs carefully in the vinegar water for about 5 minutes.

○ Remove with a skimming ladle and cool in cold water.

○ Place on a cloth and trim with a knife or scissors.

○ Arrange three thin slices of salmon in the centre of each plate and sprinkle with lemon juice.

○ Arrange two lettuce leaves attractively on top of the salmon.

○ Season with salt and pepper.

○ Place an egg in the centre of each circle of lettuce, and garnish with the paprika and dill.

○ Mix all the sauce ingredients together well, and serve separately.

POTTED SCOTTISH SALMON TERRINE WITH VEGETABLES

Terrine de saumon d'Ecosse fantaisie

It is not necessary to serve a sauce with this terrine, although one is included in the recipe.

4 PEOPLE

900g (2 lb)	fresh fillet of salmon, skinned and cut into thin escalopes
550ml (1 pt)	fish stock (see page 31)
30ml (2 tbsp)	white herb vinegar
	juice of $\frac{1}{2}$ lemon
200g (7 oz)	broccoli, cut into tiny florets, and stalk diced
350g (12 oz)	spinach, thick stalks removed and washed
225g (8 oz)	carrots, peeled and cooked until just tender
6	tomatoes, skinned, seeded and diced
6	leaves of gelatine
	fresh chives and carrot leaves or dill to garnish

Sauce

425ml ($\frac{3}{4}$ pt)	low-fat natural yoghurt
15ml (1 tbsp)	English mustard
30ml (2 tbsp)	freshly cut dill
	salt and freshly ground pepper

○ Lightly poach the salmon escalopes in the stock, with the vinegar and lemon juice, for 1–2 minutes. Drain and cool. Strain the stock and reserve.

○ Blanch the broccoli in boiling, salted water. Drain and cool in iced water.

○ Blanch the spinach and cool as above.

○ Cut the carrots into strips lengthways.

○ Arrange alternate layers of salmon and vegetables, including the tomato dice, in a 1.5 litre (2$\frac{1}{2}$ pt) terrine dish.

○ Dissolve the gelatine in about one-quarter of the fish stock over a gentle heat. Add remaining stock. Chill until the consistency of unbeaten egg white, then pour into the terrine. Chill until set.

○ To make the sauce, mix all the ingredients together, then chill.

○ Serve the terrine in slices, garnished with chosen herbs. Hand the sauce separately.

TURBOT TARTARE WITH TOFU

Tartare de turbot au tofu

The fish is marinated in lemon juice, not cooked, so make sure that it is of
the best quality and as fresh as possible. The tomatoes can be served as a
canapé as well as an hors d'oeuvre.

4 PEOPLE

225g (8 oz)	fillet of turbot
60ml (4 tbsp)	lemon juice
50g (2 oz)	shallots, finely chopped
15ml (1 tbsp)	chopped parsley
1	radish, peeled and finely grated
25g (1 oz)	tofu
8	medium tomatoes
225g (8 oz)	cucumber
	cut dill
	pinch of Cayenne
	salt and freshly ground pepper

○ Remove any bones from the fish and then chop the flesh very finely. Place in a basin
with 45ml (3 tbsp) of the lemon juice. Leave for about 30 minutes.

○ Mix together the shallots, parsley and radish.

○ Beat together the remaining lemon juice and the tofu. Add the shallot mixture.

○ Check the fish to see that it is opaque all the way through, then drain and mix with
the shallot and tofu mixture. Season to taste with Cayenne, salt and pepper.

○ Remove the 'lids' from the tomatoes and scoop out the seeds. Sprinkle with salt and
pepper. Cut a piece from the base of each so that they will stand properly.

○ Drain excess liquid from the turbot. Pipe or spoon turbot into the tomatoes, then
arrange on individual plates.

○ Cut the cucumber into julienne strips and spoon around the filled tomatoes. Sprinkle
with cut dill, and serve with small pieces of wholemeal toast.

LEEK TART WITH MOZZARELLA AND APPLES

Tarte de poireaux au Mozzarella et pommes fruits

Other cheeses can be used instead of Mozzarella – Raclette and Edam, for instance.

8 PEOPLE

450g (1 lb)	young leeks, washed well and cut into 1cm (½ in) rings
8	basil leaves, cut into fine strips
225g (8 oz)	potatoes, washed, peeled and cut into slices 6mm (¼ in) thick
200g (7 oz)	filo paste, rolled out thinly (see page 38)
175g (6 oz)	Mozzarella cheese, diced
1	cooking apple, peeled, cored and cut into small pieces
	salt and freshly ground pepper

○ Heat a non-stick pan and sauté the leek rings for about 10 minutes, turning constantly, until they are soft.

○ Season with salt, pepper and basil.

○ Cook the potato slices in a little water until just soft, about 7–8 minutes. Allow to cool.

○ Divide the very thin filo paste into four squares, about 30 × 30cm (12 × 12 in).

○ Place three pieces of paste on a non-stick baking sheet. Arrange alternate layers of potato and leek on top.

○ Sprinkle over the Mozzarella dice and then finally the pieces of apple.

○ Top with remaining sheet of filo paste and seal edges. Prick several times with a fork and bake slowly in the oven, at 160°C/325°F/Gas 3, for about 30 minutes.

○ The tart should be baked very slowly. If the top starts to brown too quickly, reduce the heat or cover loosely with foil. Serve it warm.

STUFFED COURGETTE FLOWERS
WITH RED PEPPER SAUCE

Fleurs de courgettes farcies à la sauce de piments doux

4 PEOPLE

150g (5 oz)	fillet of pike (or other white fish), skinned and boned
1	egg white
150g (5 oz)	fromage blanc (see page 33)
4	courgettes with their flowers
200ml (7 fl. oz)	fish stock (see page 31)
	salt and freshly ground pepper

Red pepper sauce

2	medium red peppers
15ml (1 tbsp)	finely chopped shallots
1	small clove of garlic, skinned and chopped
	a few sprigs of fresh thyme
400ml (14 fl. oz)	fish stock (see page 31)
	a pinch of sugar
	salt and freshly ground pepper

○ To make the sauce, wash and trim the peppers and cut into large pieces. Sweat the shallots and garlic in a non-stick pan over gentle heat, without browning. Add the red peppers and thyme.

○ Add the fish stock and simmer, uncovered, for about 20 minutes until the peppers are tender. Liquidize and season to taste with sugar, salt and pepper.

○ Purée the pike fillet in a food processor until smooth. Add the egg white and a pinch of salt and pepper, and purée again until well mixed. Transfer the mixture to a bowl.

○ Beat in the fromage blanc, a little at a time, with a wooden spoon. Season to taste.

○ Place the bowl in a larger bowl of ice for about 15 minutes.

○ Meanwhile wash and dry the courgettes very carefully.

○ Place the chilled pike mousse in a piping bag (or use a teaspoon), and carefully fill the courgette flowers.

○ Make even cuts in courgettes almost to the flower (see photograph opposite page 49).

○ Steam the courgettes over the fish stock for 3–4 minutes.

○ Spoon a little warm red pepper sauce on to each of four plates, place the courgettes on top, and serve at once.

CRAB CRESCENTS DORCHESTER

Croissants de crabe Dorchester

4 PEOPLE

25g (1 oz)	shallots, finely chopped
300g (11 oz)	white crab meat, without shell
$\frac{1}{2}$	clove of garlic, skinned and freshly crushed
5ml (1 tsp)	freshly cut basil
1	quantity of ravioli paste (see page 39)
1	egg, beaten lightly
200ml (7 fl. oz)	tomato coulis (see page 119)
60ml (4 tbsp)	freshly grated Parmesan cheese
	salt and freshly ground pepper
12	basil leaves to garnish

○ Sweat the shallots carefully in a non-stick pan without browning.

○ Add the crab meat and stir well.

○ Add the garlic, cut basil, and salt and pepper to taste. Leave to get cold.

○ Roll out the ravioli paste very thinly on a lightly floured surface to a rectangle about 23 × 15cm (9 × 6 in). Cut out twenty-four squares about 4cm (1½ in) each, then cut each square into two triangles.

○ Brush the edge of each triangle with beaten egg.

○ Place a small amount of filling on each triangle and roll up, from the longest edge, bringing the ends round to make a crescent shape. Press lightly to enclose filling.

○ Cook the crescents in boiling salted water for 4–5 minutes. Drain well.

○ Mix with hot tomato coulis, then arrange on a suitable dish and sprinkle with grated Parmesan.

○ Brown under the grill, then serve immediately, garnished with fresh basil leaves.

CRAB TERRINE WITH AVOCADO SAUCE

Terrine de crabe, sauce aux avocats

15 PEOPLE

200g (7 oz)	smoked salmon, sliced thinly
4	eggs
450g (1 lb)	quark (see page 34)
450g (1 lb)	cooked white crab meat (carefully checked to remove any small pieces of shell)
150g (5 oz)	cucumber
300g (11 oz)	tomatoes, skinned, seeded and cut into small dice
30ml (2 tbsp)	freshly cut chives
	freshly ground pepper
15	cherry tomatoes to serve

Avocado sauce

2	medium, ripe avocados
	juice of $\frac{1}{2}$ lemon
150g (5 oz)	low-fat natural yoghurt
	salt and freshly ground pepper

○ Line a 1.5 litre (2½ pt) terrine (for example, a foil container) with slices of smoked salmon, leaving a little to cover the top.

○ Whisk the eggs, and mix in the quark and crab meat.

○ Cut the cucumber into four lengthways, and remove the seeds. Cut into small dice.

○ Add cucumber, tomatoes and chives to the crab mixture. Season with pepper only.

○ Transfer the mixture to the salmon-lined terrine, fold over any pieces of smoked salmon, and top with the reserved slices. Cover with foil.

○ Poach in a bain-marie (or a roasting tin filled with hot water) in the oven at 160°C/325°F/Gas 3 for about 1¼-1½ hours until a skewer comes out clean and warm if pressed into the centre.

○ Remove from the bain-marie and allow to go cold, then turn out on to a suitable dish.

○ To make the sauce, peel the avocados and remove the stones. Push through a sieve, then mix in the remaining ingredients. Season to taste.

○ To serve, remove the tops from the cherry tomatoes, scoop out the seeds and fill with a little avocado sauce. Arrange a slice of terrine on each plate and garnish with a tomato and a little extra sauce.

WILD MUSHROOM TERRINE WITH CHIVES

Terrine de champignons sauvages à la ciboulette

In the picture opposite we have used a mushroom-shaped mould, but any
terrine dish can be used – if less wittily! Any mushrooms can be used if
some of those below are not available.

15 PEOPLE

150g (5 oz)	chanterelles (girolles)
150g (5 oz)	oyster mushrooms (pleurottes), sliced
150g (5 oz)	cèpes, sliced
150g (5 oz)	button mushrooms, sliced
100g (4 oz)	horn of plenty mushrooms (trompettes)
100g (4 oz)	St George's mushrooms (mousserons)
6	leaves of gelatine, soaked in cold water until soft, and squeezed dry
500ml (18 fl. oz)	white chicken stock (see page 23)
60ml (4 tbsp)	freshly cut chives
300g (11 oz)	fromage blanc (see page 33)
	paprika
	salt and freshly ground pepper
	fresh chives to garnish

○ Trim and clean the mushrooms, then wash and dry well. Sauté in a non-stick frying
   pan over high heat, then allow to cool. Season to taste with salt and pepper.

○ Dissolve the gelatine in about one-quarter of the warm stock, then add the remaining
   stock.

○ Chill the stock until the consistency of unbeaten egg white.

○ Stir in the mushrooms and cut chives and transfer to a 1.5 litre (2½ pt) terrine dish.

○ Cover and chill until set.

○ To serve, cut into slices and arrange each slice on a plate with a small quenelle of
   seasoned fromage blanc sprinkled with paprika and a few short lengths of fresh
   chives.

Wild Mushroom Terrine with Chives (see page 64)

Mixed Noodles (see page 72)

MARINATED SCOTCH FILLET OF BEEF JAPANESE STYLE

Filet de boeuf mariné à la japonaise

These paper-thin, raw beef slices are served with leeks in a dressing which
needs no further salt because of the salt in the soya sauce.

4 PEOPLE

225g (8 oz)	fillet of Scotch beef without fat
	juice of 1 lemon
175g (6 oz)	leek, white part only,
	cut into 4cm (1¾ in) lengths
75g (3 oz)	oyster mushrooms
100g (4 oz)	curly endive and oak leaf lettuce,
	washed and dried well
	salt and freshly ground pepper

Dressing

30ml (2 tbsp)	sherry vinegar
30ml (2 tbsp)	white wine vinegar
90ml (6 tbsp)	soya sauce
	freshly ground pepper

○ Cut the beef fillet into thin slices and, layered between sheets of plastic film, carefully beat until extremely thin.

○ Sprinkle the meat with about half the lemon juice, and some salt and pepper.

○ Cook the leek with remaining lemon juice and some salt in boiling water until just tender, then drain.

○ Mix together the dressing ingredients, then marinate the leeks while still warm.

○ Season the oyster mushrooms with salt and pepper and sauté them quickly until brown in a non-stick pan.

○ Arrange the dry salad leaves and the leek on individual serving plates, and carefully arrange the thin meat slices on top.

○ Garnish with the still warm oyster mushrooms and serve immediately.

MOSAIC OF SEASONAL VEGETABLES

Mosaïque de légumes à ma façon

It is vital for this recipe to blanch the vegetables to the *al dente* stage only. They must still be crunchy in order to keep their flavour and texture during the later poaching process. To retain maximum flavour, cool them quickly in their own stock surrounded by ice, or in some cold vegetable stock over ice. Different vegetables can be used according to season, but they should all be chosen for colour and texture, so that they contribute to the attractiveness of the finished dish.

15 PEOPLE

4	globe artichokes
	juice of $1\frac{1}{2}$ lemons
3	bunches of watercress, well washed and stalks removed
4	eggs, beaten
450g (1 lb)	fromage blanc (see page 33)
225g (8 oz)	small carrots, peeled, blanched, and cut in quarters, lengthwise
500g (1 lb, 2 oz)	broccoli, cleaned, blanched and divided into florets
100g (4 oz)	mangetout, topped, tailed and blanched
100g (4 oz)	tiny green beans, topped, tailed and blanched
200g (7 oz)	small courgettes, blanched and cut in quarters lengthwise
300g (11 oz)	chanterelles (or any other mushroom)
	salt and freshly ground pepper

○ Break off the stems of the artichokes and cut away three-quarters of the leafy head.

○ Remove the remaining leaves from the artichoke bottoms and scrape out the choke.

○ Blanch the bottoms in boiling salted water with the juice of 1 lemon for 3 minutes. Drain and place in fresh boiling salted water with the remaining lemon juice. Cook until just tender, about 10–12 minutes.

○ Allow to cool in the water, sitting in a bowl of ice. Slice the artichoke bottoms.

○ Blanch the watercress in boiling salted water. Drain, cool, then purée until smooth.

○ Mix the eggs with the fromage blanc.

○ Stir the puréed watercress into one-third of the cheese mixture.

○ Line the base of a 1.5 litre ($2\frac{1}{2}$ pt) terrine dish with non-stick paper. Spoon the watercress mixture into the terrine and level the surface.

○ Arrange the carrots on top in an even layer.

○ Continue layering up the vegetables with a thin layer of plain cheese mixture between each vegetable layer.

○ Cover with foil and poach in a bain-marie (or roasting tin filled with hot water) at 160°C/325°F/Gas 3 for about 1 hour until a skewer pressed into the centre comes out clean and warm.

○ Remove from the bain-marie, cool and then chill until required. Serve in slices. As it is quite moist, the terrine does not require a sauce.

STEAMED RED MULLET FILLETS WITH VEGETABLES

Rouget à la vapeur et légumes

4 PEOPLE

4	red mullet, about 175g (6 oz) each, filleted and boned
1	carrot, peeled
2	button onions
15ml (1 tbsp)	lemon juice
15ml (1 tbsp)	white wine vinegar
30ml (2 tbsp)	reduced fish stock (see page 31)
	salt and freshly ground pepper
16	pieces of fresh chives, cut into 5cm (2 in) strips

○ Season the red mullet fillets and place skin side up on greaseproof paper.

○ Cut the carrot with a cannelle knife, then slice into paper-thin rounds.

○ Cut the onions into fine rings.

○ Blanch the carrot and onion in boiling water until just tender, about 1–2 minutes.

○ Sprinkle fish fillets with the carrot and onion, and steam for 3–5 minutes.

○ Heat the lemon juice and vinegar. Whisk in the stock; season with salt and pepper.

○ Arrange the fish fillets on a plate, spoon over the sauce and garnish with cut chives.

OYSTER SAUSAGES
WITH SAFFRON AND INK SAUCES

Saucisses des huîtres 'jaune et noir'

This dish was created for a gathering of eighteen chefs voted the world's best in a recent book. It took place in The Dorchester's Terrace Restaurant and, not unnaturally, I was trying to create something very unusual, with exciting flavours, colours and textures.

4 PEOPLE

200g (7 oz)	salmon trout, skinned and boned
100g (4 oz)	tofu
24	oysters
10ml (2 tsp)	finely cut dill
	juice of $\frac{1}{2}$ lemon
40-50cm (16–20 in)	sausage skins, soaked in water
	salt and freshly ground pepper

Saffron sauce

400ml (14 fl. oz)	fish stock (see page 31)
30g ($1\frac{1}{4}$ oz)	shallots, finely chopped
	a few strands of saffron
100g (4 oz)	fromage blanc (see page 33)
	salt and freshly ground pepper

Ink sauce

500g (1 lb. 2 oz)	fresh squid *with ink*
25g (1 oz)	shallots, finely chopped
50g (2 oz)	tomatoes, diced
300ml ($\frac{1}{2}$ pt)	fish stock (see page 31)
	salt and freshly ground pepper

Garnish

8	crayfish, poached for 2 minutes, tails removed
200g (7 oz)	tiny broccoli florets, washed and blanched for 15 seconds

○ To make the sausages, purée the salmon trout in a food processor. Chill in a bowl over ice, and gradually beat in the tofu, a little at a time. Season well and chill until required.

○ Open the oysters, take oysters from shells carefully, saving their liquid.

○ Mix oysters with dill and chilled salmon trout mousse, and, if necessary, season with lemon juice, salt and pepper.

○ Put mixture of mousse and whole oysters into a piping bag, and fill the sausage skins. Tie with string to make four sausages. Chill until required.

○ To make the saffron sauce, put fish stock and shallots into a pan, and reduce stock by half by rapid boiling.

○ Add the saffron and fromage blanc, and mix in well.

○ Bring to the boil again and pass through a fine sieve. Season to taste.

○ To make the squid sauce, remove the ink sacs from the bodies of the fish. Separate the heads from the bodies and wash well (save the meat for another dish).

○ Sweat the finely chopped shallots in a non-stick pan. Add the ink pouches, squid heads and tomatoes, and sweat for a further 3–4 minutes.

○ Add fish stock and oyster liquor, cover and simmer for 5 minutes. Pass through a fine sieve, boil up again and season with salt and pepper.

○ Poach the oyster sausages in water for 3 minutes, and sauté broccoli and crayfish tails quickly in a non-stick pan.

○ To serve, pour the hot yellow saffron sauce gently on to half of each of four individual plates. Cover the other half of the plate with the hot black squid sauce. Place the oyster sausages in the middle of the two sauces, where they meet. Garnish with the warm, seasoned crayfish and broccoli florets.

○ Instead of sausage skins, wrap the sausage mixture in soaked caul fat for a softer casing, and then grill rather than poach.

RAVIOLI WITH SPINACH AND PARSLEY SAUCE

Ravioli aux épinards et sauce persil

4 PEOPLE

25g (1 oz)	shallots, finely chopped
225g (8 oz)	fresh spinach leaves, well washed, thick stalks removed, and blanched
1	clove of garlic, skinned and crushed
1	egg, beaten
50g (2 oz)	cottage cheese
1	quantity of ravioli paste (see page 39)
	a pinch of grated nutmeg
	salt and freshly ground pepper
	beaten egg to seal

Parsley sauce

200g (7 oz)	flat leaf parsley, stems removed
40g (1½ oz)	shallots, finely chopped
300ml (½ pt)	white veal stock (see page 24)
50g (2 oz)	fromage blanc (see page 33)
	juice of ½ lemon
	salt and freshly ground pepper

○ Sauté the shallots in a non-stick pan without browning.

○ Chop the spinach finely and add to the shallots with the garlic. Cook for 1–2 minutes.

○ Remove from the heat and beat in the egg, cheese and seasonings.

○ Roll out half the ravioli paste until thin, then arrange teaspoonfuls of the mixture at regular intervals about 2.5cm (1 in) apart.

○ Brush between each spoonful of filling with beaten egg.

○ Roll out the other half of paste to a similar size and carefully place on top of the first.

○ Press firmly between the filling to make each square of ravioli. Cut in between each one with a sharp knife.

○ To make the sauce, place parsley leaves in a saucepan with the shallots and half the stock. Bring to the boil, reduce heat, cover and simmer for 5 minutes.

○ Add the fromage blanc and lemon juice and liquidize, adding the remaining stock gradually to give the required consistency – nice and runny. Season to taste with salt and pepper.

○ Cook ravioli in boiling salted water for 3–4 minutes. Drain, rinse in boiling water, and serve at once with hot parsley sauce.

TORTELLINI WITH BEETROOT FILLING

Tortellini farci à la betterave

Using a double quantity of ravioli paste, make these tortellini in whatever colour you like – black, red, green, brown or white – and freeze any remainder. *Mix* the colours, too, if preferred.

To vary the tortellini shape, you could cut out 6cm (2¼ in) squares instead of circles. Place 5ml (1 tsp) of filling in the middle of each square and brush the edges with egg white. Press diagonally opposite corners together over the filling, then press down the other facing corners in the same way. Press all edges together so that the filling is completely enclosed. Cook as below.

10 PEOPLE

2	quantities of ravioli paste (see page 39)

Filling

100g (4 oz)	beetroot, cooked and peeled
100g (4 oz)	carrots, cooked
100g (4 oz)	celery, cooked
1	slice of wholewheat bread, without crust, about 30g (1¼ oz), soaked in 50ml (2 fl. oz) hot water and squeezed out
1	egg, separated
20g (¾ oz)	chives, finely cut
50g (2 oz)	fromage blanc (see page 33)
2-3	sage leaves, finely cut
5ml (1 tsp)	poppy seeds
1	clove of garlic, skinned and finely chopped
100g (4 oz)	Parmesan cheese, freshly grated
	salt and freshly ground pepper

○ To make the filling, cut the beetroot, carrot and celery into cubes and purée with the brown bread in the liquidizer.

○ Add the egg yolk and chives, mix and season to taste with salt and pepper.

○ Roll out the dough thinly on a floured surface and cut out 6cm (2¼ in) circles.

○ Place 5ml (1 tsp) of the filling in the middle of each circle of dough, brush the edges with the egg white, and fold the circles in half. Press the edges together well.

○ Carefully make the semicircles into circle shapes around the fingers so that both ends touch. With the other hand, bend the firmly pressed edges of the dough upwards.

○ Cook the tortellini in plenty of boiling salted water, a portion at a time, until *al dente* (until they float on top of the water), then drain in a sieve.

○ Heat the fromage blanc in a pan, and add the sage leaves, poppy seeds and garlic.

○ Add the tortellini, mix well and season to taste. Heat gently through.

○ To serve, put on to four individual plates, and sprinkle with the grated Parmesan.

HOME-MADE EGG NOODLES

Nouilles aux oeufs frais

Noodles are fairly simple to make at home and taste very superior to the bought varieties. They can be flavoured and coloured in many ways, as you can see from the suggestions below. For a stunning presentation, serve a selection of coloured noodles.
Noodles must always be cooked *al dente*. After draining, rinse with hot water, toss in a little warmed fromage blanc, season and serve immediately. Freshly cut herbs such as basil or chives may be added.

4 PEOPLE

200g (7 oz)	strong plain flour (or fine wholewheat flour), sieved
25g (1 oz)	semolina
1	egg
	a pinch of salt
45-60ml (3–4 tbsp)	hot water

○ Mix the flour and semolina together and make a well in the centre.

○ Place the other ingredients in the well.

○ Gradually work the flour and semolina in towards the middle and knead into a very firm, smooth dough.

○ Wrap in a damp cloth, and allow to rest in a cool place for at least 2–3 hours.

○ Divide the dough into five pieces and roll out each piece as thinly as possible. Lay the pieces on top of each other and cut into strips approximately 6mm ($\frac{1}{4}$ in) wide.

○ An alternative method of cutting is to roll the five pieces of dough into thin circles. Fold each circle in loosely from both sides, parallel to the middle. Do this again until both folded edges meet in the middle. Then cut the dough into strips.

○ These noodles may be cooked while fresh or left to dry out. Boil for 2–3 minutes if fresh, for about double that time if dried.

○ If wholewheat flour is used instead of plain, the pasta will be brown, not white.

HOME-MADE EGG NOODLES WITH INK

Nouilles à l'encre

200g (7 oz)	strong plain flour, sieved
25g (1 oz)	semolina
1	egg
	a pinch of salt
40ml (8 tsp)	reduced squid ink, plus a little warm water if necessary (see page 73)

Buy very fresh squid with unbroken ink sacs, so that as much ink as possible can be collected. About 1kg (2¼ lb) squid should provide enough ink to reduce, by simmering, to the required quantity of 40ml (8 tsp). If necessary, make the amount up with a little warm water. (Use the squid meat in Squid Salad, see page 45.)

Add ink, or ink and water, to the flour mixture instead of the hot water in the recipe for Home-Made Egg Noodles, along with the egg.

HOME-MADE EGG NOODLES WITH SAFFRON

Nouilles au safran

200g (7 oz)	strong plain flour, sieved
25g (1 oz)	semolina
1	egg
	a pinch of salt
	a large pinch of saffron strands
	or powder

Blanch the saffron in 45-60ml (3-4 tbsp) hot water. When a deep yellow, add the strained liquid to the flour mixture instead of the hot water in the recipe for Home-Made Egg Noodles, along with the egg.

HOME-MADE EGG NOODLES WITH SPINACH

Nouilles aux épinards

200g (7 oz)	strong plain flour, sieved
25g (1 oz)	semolina
1	egg
	a pinch of salt
50g (2 oz)	spinach purée, plus
	a little warm water if necessary

Wash about 300g (11 oz) spinach leaves thoroughly and cut away thick stalks. Blanch quickly, then refresh in cold water. Chop very finely or purée in a blender or liquidizer. Add 50g (2 oz) of this purée, with a little warm water if necessary, to the flour mixture instead of the hot water in the recipe for Home-Made Egg Noodles, along with the egg.

HOME-MADE EGG NOODLES WITH TOMATO

Nouilles aux tomates

200g (7 oz)	strong plain white flour, sieved
25g (1 oz)	semolina
1	egg
	a pinch of salt
50g (2 oz)	tomato coulis (see page 119)

Add the tomato coulis, with a little warm water if necessary, to the flour mixture instead of the hot water in the recipe for Home-Made Egg Noodles, along with the egg.

SOUPS

Soups are becoming fashionable again after many years of apparent culinary disfavour. It is a welcome reappearance, because soups can be good for health, can look and taste spectacular, and are very versatile. A bowl of a vegetable soup or chowder could be a light lunch - with some wholewheat bread as the ideal healthy accompaniment - or the first course of a simpler two- or three-course meal; a perfectly clear consommé garnished with colourful vegetable dice and medallions of seafood could be served after the hors d'oeuvre and before the main course. A cold soup is the perfect start to a meal on a hot day.

The soups in this brief chapter - ranging from the most sophisticated lobster consommé to a nourishing, protein-rich lentil soup - encompass *par excellence* all the principles of Cuisine Naturelle: using the best ingredients, and made without butter, oil, cream, or alcohol.

The basis of any good soup, though, is the best stock, and, although many of the soup recipes hold instructions for their own individual stock or consommé, there are inevitable cross-references to the chapter on stocks.

To cut down on salt, a relevant herb mixture from the selection on page 40 could be used instead of some salt in all the soup recipes.

COLD VEGETABLE SOUP
WITH BASIL

Potage froid des meilleurs légumes du potager

4 PEOPLE

900g (2 lb)	ripe red tomatoes, seeded and diced
200g (7 oz)	cucumber, seeded and diced
50g (2 oz)	onion, finely diced
50g (2 oz)	red pepper, cored and diced
1	clove of garlic, skinned and crushed
25g (1 oz)	fresh brown breadcrumbs
40ml (8 tsp)	red wine vinegar
225ml (8 fl. oz)	vegetable stock (see page 30)
	a few sprigs of oregano
16	basil leaves
	salt and freshly ground pepper

○ Mix together the tomatoes, cucumber, onion, red pepper, garlic and breadcrumbs.

○ Add the vinegar, stock, oregano and twelve of the basil leaves.

○ Marinate for 12 hours.

○ Liquidize to a purée, and season to taste.

○ Serve cold, garnished with the remaining basil leaves.

DIALOGUE OF FRUIT PUREES

Dialogue de purées de fruits

This marbling of purées looks spectacular. It can be served in summer as a
first-course soup, as a sorbet in between courses, or as a dessert.
The idea was created by the famous German chef, Hans Peter Wodarz,
who is a great friend.

4 PEOPLE

225g (8 oz)	kiwi fruit, peeled
400g (14 oz)	mangoes, peeled and stoned
200g (7 oz)	strawberries, cleaned
200g (7 oz)	blackcurrants, cleaned and stemmed
250g (9 oz)	apples, peeled and cored
200g (7 oz)	raspberries
	juice of $\frac{1}{2}$ lemon
100ml (4 fl. oz)	mineral water
	a little caster sugar
	a little apple juice
	wild strawberries (or raspberries) and
	tiny sprigs of mint for garnish

○ Carefully crush the kiwi fruit with a fork (the black pips should not be broken).
Remove pips and strain the purée through a fine sieve. Thin down a little with mineral
water if necessary. Chill.

○ Purée the mango flesh in the liquidizer. Strain as above, and thin down with mineral
water if necessary. Chill.

○ Purée the strawberries in the liquidizer, strain as above, and season well with a little
lemon juice and sugar. Chill.

○ Bring the blackcurrants to the boil in water with a little lemon juice and sugar. Allow
to cool, then purée and strain through a fine sieve. Thin with a little mineral water if
necessary. Chill.

○ Cook the apples until very soft in a minimum of water with a little lemon juice and
sugar. Allow to cool then strain through a fine sieve. If necessary thin the purée down
with a little apple juice so that it has the same consistency as the kiwi purée. Chill.

○ Purée the raspberries in a liquidizer and strain through a fine sieve. Strengthen the
raspberry flavour with lemon juice and sugar. If necessary, thin down with mineral
water. Chill.

○ To serve, put a scoop of each very cold purée into a soup plate, arranging them around
the plate, with the darkest one in the middle (see colour plates, pages 88–9). Knock
the plate firmly (not *too* firmly, or you may break it) on a solid surface, so that the
purées blend together at the edges. Garnish with a wild strawberry and mint.

FISHERMAN'S CLAM CHOWDER

This chowder can also be served cold.

4 PEOPLE

24	cherrystone clams
750ml (1¼ pt)	fish stock (see page 31)
25g (1 oz)	onion ⎫
25g (1 oz)	leek ⎬ cut in small dice
25g (1 oz)	carrot ⎪
50g (2 oz)	celeriac ⎭
1	clove of garlic, skinned and crushed
1	small bay leaf
25g (1 oz)	green pepper, cut in small dice
100g (4 oz)	potato, peeled and cut in small dice
2	tomatoes, halved, seeded and diced
5ml (1 tsp)	chopped fresh thyme
5ml (1 tsp)	chopped parsley
	salt and freshly ground pepper

○ Scrub the clams and place in a large pan with the stock. Cover and simmer until the clams open. Remove from the stock and leave to cool. Strain the stock through muslin or a fine sieve and reserve.

○ Remove the hard white tendon from the clams and chop the flesh.

○ Sauté the onion, leek, carrot, celeriac and garlic in a non-stick pan without browning.

○ Add the bay leaf, green pepper, potato and reserved stock, and simmer for about 5 minutes.

○ Add the clams and the tomatoes and simmer for a further 5 minutes. Remove bay leaf.

○ Add herbs, and season to taste with salt and pepper.

FISH SOUP WITH CRAB AND MELON

Bouillon de poissons au crabe et melon

Only the white meat of the crab is used for this soup and you can keep the brown meat for use in another dish: dressed crab, crab salads, or canapé toppings. The crab-flavoured court bouillon can be kept, too, for another dish (best frozen). I used Honeydew melon for the soup, but any melon in season is suitable.

4 PEOPLE

1	crab, about 800g (1¾ lb)
4 litres (7 pt)	court bouillon (see page 32)
1.2 litres (good 2 pt)	clear fish stock (see page 31)
10ml (2 tsp)	soya sauce
	freshly ground pepper
225g (8 oz)	ripe melon flesh
4	thin slices of peeled lemon
	fresh coriander or chervil leaves

○ Brush and wash the crab, put into boiling court bouillon, and cook for 10 minutes.

○ Allow to cool in the court bouillon, then break open the crab and carefully remove the meats.

○ Slowly reduce the fish stock by half, then season with the soya sauce and freshly ground pepper. Strain through a fine cloth.

○ Cut the melon flesh into small pieces of equal size or use a melon-baller.

○ Warm the white crab meat and pieces of melon in a little stock, then arrange in suitable soup dishes.

○ Pour in the well-seasoned fish stock. Add the lemon slices and serve immediately, garnished with coriander or chervil leaves.

CRAYFISH AND CHICKEN SOUP WITH CHERVIL

Petite marmite d'écrevisses et de volaille

4 PEOPLE

2	raw chicken carcasses, with giblets
100g (4 oz)	*each* of onion, carrot, leek and celery, half in dice and half in fine julienne strips
1	sprig of thyme
1	sprig of rosemary
1.5 litres (2½ pt)	water
16	live crayfish
1	chicken breast, skinned and boned
	salt and freshly ground pepper
	small bunch of chervil to garnish

○ Roughly chop the chicken carcasses and place in a large pan.

○ Add the diced vegetables with the thyme, rosemary and water. Bring to the boil, reduce heat, then simmer for 1 hour.

○ Meanwhile, blanch the crayfish for 1 minute in a minimum of boiling salted water. Leave in the cooking liquid, but place pan in a bowl of ice.

○ When cool, remove the tails from the crayfish. Reserve and roughly chop all the shells.

○ Strain the chicken stock through a fine cloth and remove any fat. Return to a clean saucepan.

○ Poach the crayfish tails in the stock for 2 minutes, then remove from the pan.

○ Add the crushed shells to the stock and simmer for 10 minutes.

○ Strain the stock into a clean pan and poach the chicken breast for 5 minutes until just pink. Remove from the pan.

○ Add the julienne of vegetables to the pan and cook for 1 minute.

○ Cut the chicken breast into julienne strips, then add to the pan along with the crayfish tails.

○ Warm through, without boiling. Check seasoning then serve at once, garnished with sprigs of chervil.

SCALLOP SOUP
FLAVOURED WITH GINGER

Potage aux coquilles St-Jacques parfumé au gingembre

4 PEOPLE

12	scallops in their shells
25g (1 oz)	fresh ginger root
2	large spring onions
550ml (1 pt)	fish stock (see page 31)
15ml (1 tbsp)	soya sauce
2.5ml ($\frac{1}{2}$ tsp)	arrowroot
	a squeeze of lemon juice
	salt and freshly ground pepper

○ Open the scallops with a strong knife and lay them on a warm hot-plate (or in a hot frying pan) for a few minutes until they open completely. Remove the white flesh and coral with a soup spoon. Carefully separate the white flesh from the coral and wash quickly.

○ Cut the scallops into strips 3mm ($\frac{1}{8}$ in) thick.

○ Peel the ginger and reserve the trimmings. Cut the ginger into fine julienne strips. Place in cold water, bring to the boil, drain and reserve.

○ Finely slice the spring onions.

○ Place the ginger trimmings in the fish stock. Bring to the boil and leave to infuse for 15 minutes. Strain through fine cheesecloth into a clean pan.

○ Add the soya sauce, julienne of ginger and shredded spring onions to the strained stock, and bring to simmering point.

○ Mix the arrowroot with a little water and stir into the stock. Season to taste with lemon juice, salt and pepper.

○ Season the scallops and coral. Add the coral to the soup and poach for 20 seconds. Add the strips of scallop and poach for a further 10 seconds. Serve at once.

LOBSTER CONSOMME WITH CORIANDER LEAVES

Consommé de homard aux feuilles de coriandre

This is a very unusual consommé but well worth the effort – it is a wonderful combination in both flavour and colour. Female lobsters are used, because they are much more flavourful and because the coral and eggs are used in the garnish.

10 PEOPLE

2	live female lobsters, about 350g (12 oz) each
3 litres (5¼ pt)	court bouillon (see page 32)

Basic stock

1.5kg (3¼ lb)	lobster shells, chopped, with claws and body meat
150g (5 oz)	leeks
100g (4 oz)	carrots
100g (4 oz)	celery } cut in small cubes
100g (4 oz)	tomatoes
50g (2 oz)	onions
1	clove
5 litres (8¾ pt)	fish stock (see page 31)
	salt

To clarify

500g (1 lb, 2 oz)	white fish fillet, skinned, boned and minced
100g (4 oz)	tomatoes
100g (4 oz)	leeks
65g (2½ oz)	celery } cut in small cubes
65g (2½ oz)	carrot
6	coriander stalks
3	tarragon stalks
2	egg whites, whisked until frothy
200g (7 oz)	ice cubes

Garnish

20	small lobster medallions (cut from tails of above)
150g (5 oz)	*each* of celery and carrot, thinly sliced and cut into lobster shapes, then blanched in lightly salted water for 15 seconds
30-40	enoki mushrooms
20-30	fresh coriander leaves
40g (1½ oz)	lobster eggs, blanched in a minimum of water with 15ml (1 tbsp) vinegar added

○ Splash the live lobsters with cold water, then plunge into the boiling court bouillon for 2 minutes. Remove from heat and leave to cool in court bouillon, the pan sitting in a large bowl of ice to speed up the process.

○ Shell the lobsters and retain meat for garnish. Put shells on a tray in a moderate oven (180°C/350°F/Gas 4) for about 20 minutes until dry. This helps to bring out the flavour.

○ Place lobster shells and all remaining ingredients for the basic stock in a large saucepan or casserole.

○ Bring to the boil, skimming from time to time. Allow to simmer for 45 minutes, still skimming occasionally.

○ Pass carefully through a sieve and allow to cool.

○ To clarify the stock, mix all the ingredients together with the ice cubes.

○ Place in a large saucepan and add the stock. Bring to the boil, whisking constantly, and then allow to simmer for 45 minutes.

○ Pass through a fine muslin-lined sieve and season to taste with salt and pepper.

○ Pour the consommé into soup plates or cups and garnish with the lobster medallions, carrot and celery shapes, enoki mushrooms, coriander leaves and lobster eggs. Serve immediately.

POTATO AND WATERCRESS SOUP WITH MUSSELS

Potage au cresson et moules

4 PEOPLE

40g (1½ oz)	shallots, skinned and finely chopped
1	clove of garlic, skinned and finely chopped
1	medium leek, washed and finely cut
300g (11 oz)	raw potatoes, peeled and diced
2	bunches of fresh watercress, tough stalks removed
500ml (18 fl. oz)	strong fish stock (see page 31)
500ml (18 fl. oz)	strong white chicken stock (see page 23)

For the mussels

500g (1 lb, 2 oz)	mussels
50g (2 oz)	leek
50g (2 oz)	carrots ⎫ finely cut
50g (2 oz)	celery ⎭
1	sprig of thyme
1	clove of garlic, unskinned and crushed
150ml (¼ pt)	fish stock (see page 31)

○ Sweat the shallots and garlic gently in a non-stick pan.

○ Add the leek, potatoes and watercress leaves, reserving twelve leaves for garnish.

○ Sweat until soft without allowing the ingredients to brown, then add the stocks and boil up once.

○ Purée the soup in the liquidizer, pour into a saucepan and season.

○ Wash the mussels thoroughly and remove the beard.

○ Sweat the cut vegetables, thyme and garlic in a large non-stick pan for about 2 minutes, then add the mussels.

○ Add the fish stock and cook until the mussels open.

○ Remove and discard the shells, and place the mussels in the puréed soup. Warm through quickly, and garnish with watercress leaves just before serving.

CHICKEN CONSOMME WITH WHITE ASPARAGUS AND BLACK TRUFFLES

Consommé de poulet aux asperges blanches et truffes noires

4 PEOPLE

2	raw chicken carcasses, about 900g (2 lb)
2	onions with skins
1.5 litres (2½ pt)	water
2	cloves
¼	bay leaf
100g (4 oz)	leek, cleaned and roughly cut
25g (1 oz)	celery, roughly cut
	juice of 1 lemon

To clarify

200g (7 oz)	raw chicken leg meat, minced
2	egg whites, whisked until frothy
1	tomato, chopped
2	sprigs of fresh tarragon

Garnish

12	small tips of white asparagus, well blanched
12	thin slices of black truffle
12	sprigs of chervil

○ Blanch the chicken carcasses in boiling water for 1 minute.

○ Remove and rinse the carcasses under cold running water.

○ Halve the onions and place the cut sides on, over or under direct heat until dark brown.

○ Add all the ingredients for the stock to the pan. Bring to the boil, reduce heat and simmer for 1½ hours.

○ Strain through a fine cloth. Return to a clean pan.

○ To clarify the stock, stir together all the ingredients and whisk into the warm stock. Bring slowly to the boil, whisking all the time. When it comes to the boil, stop whisking, reduce heat and simmer for 45 minutes.

○ Line a sieve or colander with a fine cloth and spoon the froth into it. Pour the stock through this froth. It will be completely clear. Remove fat by dragging strips of kitchen paper over the surface of the consommé.

○ Heat to serving temperature, spoon into soup plates and garnish with asparagus tips, truffle slices and tiny sprigs of chervil.

QUAIL CONSOMME WITH CHERVIL
Consommé de cailles au cerfeuil

A consommé similar to this can be made from any other game bird or chicken. The breasts for the garnish have to be pink so that they are tender.

10 PEOPLE

600g (1 lb, 5 oz)	quail and game bird carcasses, giblets and skin, chopped
300g (11 oz)	veal knuckle, chopped
5 litres (8¾ pt)	water
100g (4 oz)	onion, unpeeled, cut in half, and well browned on hot-plate or in hot pan
1	clove
½	bay leaf
100g (4 oz)	carrots ⎫
150g (5 oz)	leek ⎬ cut in small cubes
150g (5 oz)	celery ⎭
	salt

To clarify

250g (9 oz)	raw quail leg meat, coarsely minced
250g (9 oz)	poultry meat, coarsely minced
3	egg whites *or* 10 quail egg whites, whisked until frothy
100g (4 oz)	tomatoes, coarsely chopped
100g (4 oz)	celeriac, cut into small pieces
20g (¾ oz)	parsley stalks
	a few chervil stalks
	salt and freshly ground pepper

Garnish

10	quail breasts, bones removed, but skin retained
150g (5 oz)	*each* of carrots and celery, sliced thinly then cut into chicken shapes and blanched in slightly salted water for 15 seconds
10	quail egg yolks (keep separate)
80	chervil leaves

- Carefully sauté the quail and game bird bones, giblets, skin, and veal knuckle in a non-stick pan for about 15 minutes.

- Transfer to a large casserole or pan, and add the water and a pinch of salt. Bring to the boil. Skim, then allow to simmer for 20 minutes.

- Push the clove into the browned onion and add to the stock, with the bay leaf.

- Add the carrots, leek and celery.

- Simmer for a further 45 minutes, skimming from time to time.

- Strain carefully through a fine cloth, and allow stock to cool.

- To clarify the stock, mix the quail and poultry meat with the egg whites, tomatoes, celeriac, parsley and chervil stalks.

- Add all this to the stock and bring to the boil, whisking constantly. Allow to simmer for 30 minutes.

- Pass through a fine muslin-lined sieve and remove any fat with absorbent kitchen paper. Season with salt and pepper.

- Sauté the quail breasts for the garnish in a non-stick pan for about 1 minute, turning once, until still pink. Remove the skin and slice the breasts carefully.

- Pour the consommé into soup plates and garnish with the quail breast slices, vegetable garnish, raw egg yolks and chervil (8 leaves per plate). Serve immediately.

BEEF AND LENTIL SOUP

Soupe aux lentilles

Lentils are an ancient food, almost as rich in protein as soya beans. They
contain almost no fat, but have a high carbohydrate content – so a bowl of
this soup, with only a piece of good wholewheat bread as accompaniment,
makes a sustaining and nourishing meal.

4 PEOPLE

75g (3 oz)	lean shoulder of beef, cut into small dice
50g (2 oz)	onion, finely chopped
50g (2 oz)	leek, cut into strips
50g (2 oz)	carrot, diced
150g (5 oz)	brown lentils, soaked overnight
1.5 litres (2½ pt)	meat broth (see page 22)
½	bay leaf
5ml (1 tsp)	chopped fresh thyme
	salt and freshly ground pepper

○ Sauté the seasoned beef carefully in a non-stick pan until well browned on all sides.

○ Add the onion, leek and carrot and sauté, stirring occasionally, until the onion is transparent. Transfer to a saucepan.

○ Add the soaked, drained lentils, broth, bay leaf and thyme. Cover and simmer gently for about 1 hour until meat and lentils are tender.

○ Season to taste with salt and pepper, and remove bay leaf before serving.

LEEK AND ONION SOUP

Potage de poireaux et oignons

4 PEOPLE

200g (7 oz)	onions, finely chopped
200g (7 oz)	leeks, finely cut
100ml (4 fl. oz)	brown veal stock (see page 26)
550ml (1 pt)	meat broth (see page 22)
	salt and freshly ground pepper
	a little coarsely chopped
	parsley for garnish

○ Sweat the onions and leeks carefully in a non-stick pan until golden, stirring constantly. Transfer to a saucepan.

○ Add the brown veal stock and simmer for 5 minutes to reduce a little.

○ Add the meat broth and allow to simmer for 8–10 minutes longer.

○ Season with salt and pepper, and garnish with the parsley before serving.

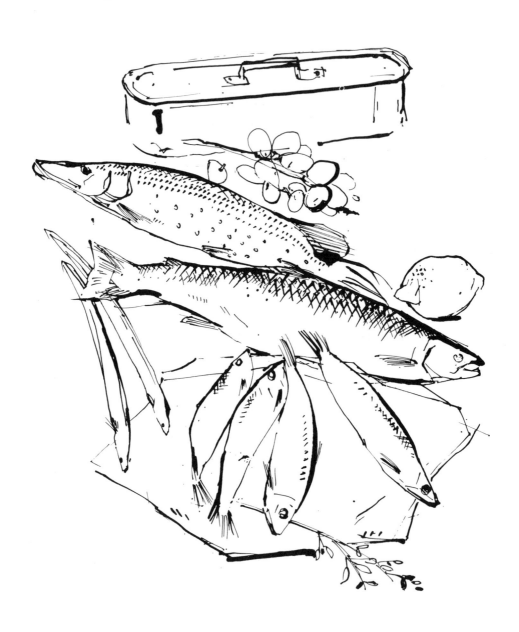

FISH

Fish has undoubtedly become the favourite ingredient of the modern creative kitchen. A fresh flavourful fish contains proteins and many of the vitamins and minerals not freely available elsewhere (Vitamin D in oily fish, and iodine, for example). Fish is also easily digested and desirable for good health. White fish, particularly, has a low fat content and contains relatively few calories.

Fish is valued too for its variety, versatility and flavour. With an increasing interest in health, and thus in fish as a major source of protein, markets should make available an enormous variety of fish throughout the country. With a few exceptions, fish come mostly from the wild. Depending on the water in which they live - and also, sadly, upon the degree of pollution in that water - their flesh develops a special character in both texture and taste. Thus there is an even wider choice. Always choose the freshest fish - look for clear eyes, red gills, firm flesh and scales. The smell from the open gills should be fresh, not 'fishy'. Try to avoid buying fish shortly before and after the spawning season (closed season) as they are then generally less tasty.

Fish is also incredibly versatile - in methods of cookery, flavour and usage - and lends itself admirably to the basics of Cuisine Naturelle - preferring indeed the processes, particularly steaming, that are central to Cuisine Naturelle. Although, in general, few sauces are used, many of the simplest vegetable sauces, natural and true in flavour, are more complementary than richer cream- or butter-based sauces.

Take care never to over-cook fish, or cook it at too high a temperature. At temperatures above 40°C/104°F, animal proteins start to coagulate, to congeal (reminiscent of the protein in eggs). At approximately 50°C/122°F, 40 to 50 per cent of the protein has congealed and at 80°C/176°F the flesh and liquid separate. This means that the flavour in the juices escapes, and the fish becomes dry and tasteless. The recipes in this chapter specify exact timings; these may appear short, but should be followed meticulously for total success.

Never leave fish soaking in water as this leaches out flavour as well as the protein, vitamins and minerals. Always use the best stocks for giving flavour to fish sauces and for poaching. The simplest of accompaniments and garnishes are all that are needed.

To cut salt consumption in the following fish recipes, try a pinch or two of the fish herb mixture on page 40: this should reduce the need for salt by about half.

STEAMED SEA BASS, CHINESE STYLE

Loup de mer à la chinoise

4 PEOPLE

1	sea bass, about 1kg (2¼ lb), cleaned
30ml (2 tbsp)	lemon juice
45ml (3 tbsp)	light soya sauce
4	spring onions, trimmed and cut into 5-7.5cm (2-3 in) lengths
10	mangetout
1	large carrot, peeled
3	cloves of garlic, skinned
1	slice of fresh root ginger, about 6mm (¼ in) thick, peeled
225ml (8 fl. oz)	fish stock (see page 31)
5ml (1 tsp)	cornflour
15-30ml (1–2 tbsp)	water
1	large egg, beaten
	freshly ground pepper

○ With a sharp knife make four or five diagonal slashes on each side of the fish.

○ Stir together 15ml (1 tbsp) each of lemon juice and soya sauce.

○ Sprinkle a little of this into each of the slashes and rub into the flesh inside and out. Season the fish with the pepper.

○ Cut the spring onion lengths into julienne and press half into the slashes in the fish. Reserve the others.

○ To prepare the sauce, cut the mangetout and carrot into julienne strips; crush the garlic and ginger; and mix together the stock, remaining lemon juice and soya sauce.

○ Steam the fish for about 10–12 minutes until the flesh along the backbone is opaque.

○ Meanwhile make the sauce. Stir together the cornflour and water. Sauté the garlic and ginger in a non-stick pan for 10 seconds, then add the reserved vegetables and cook, stirring until the colour brightens.

○ Pour in the reserved stock and water and cornflour, and cook until thickened, stirring continuously.

○ Add the egg, stirring all the time, and remove from the heat immediately.

○ Remove the fish from the steamer, transfer to a plate and spoon the sauce over. Serve at once.

SALMON TROUT STEAKS
BAKED IN THEIR OWN JUICES

Steaks de truites saumonées dans leurs jus

Always open and serve the 'packages' in front of the guests, as only then is
the taste and aroma fully appreciated.

4 PEOPLE

675g (1½ lb)	fillet of salmon trout, skinned
40g (1½ oz)	onion
50g (2 oz)	carrots
65g (2½ oz)	leek
100g (4 oz)	raw mushrooms
12	tarragon leaves
40ml (8 tsp)	fish stock (see page 31)
	salt and freshly ground pepper

onion, carrots, leek, raw mushrooms — cut into thin julienne strips

○ Carefully remove any bones from the salmon trout and cut into four steaks. Season
with salt and pepper.

○ Sweat the onion in a non-stick pan without browning until it is transparent.

○ Add the carrots and leek and continue to sweat for a further 2 minutes.

○ Finally, add the mushrooms and sweat for a further minute.

○ Add four tarragon leaves and season with salt and pepper.

○ Have ready four pieces of greaseproof paper about three times larger than each
salmon trout steak, and divide the vegetables between them.

○ Arrange the seasoned steaks on top of the vegetables and garnish with remaining
tarragon leaves.

○ Dribble a little fish stock over each steak, then carefully fold the edges together to
make an air-tight pouch.

○ Place on a baking tray, and bake in a moderate oven (325°F/160°C/Gas 3) for
8–10 minutes.

FILLET OF SCOTTISH SALMON
WITH WATERCRESS

Suprême de saumon d'Ecosse au cresson

4 PEOPLE

500g (1 lb, 2 oz)	fresh fillet of salmon, cut into 4 pieces
15g (½ oz)	shallots, chopped
250ml (9 fl. oz)	fish stock (see page 31)

Mousseline of pike

1	bunch of watercress, stalks removed
150g (5 oz)	fillet of pike (or whiting, angler or turbot), chilled
1	egg white, chilled
150g (5 oz)	fromage blanc, chilled (see page 33)
	salt and freshly ground pepper

○ For the mousseline, blanch the watercress leaves in boiling salted water. Refresh in iced water and drain well.

○ Purée the pike fillet in a food processor with the watercress, then add the egg white, a pinch of salt, and purée until thick and smooth.

○ Place the fish mixture in a basin over a bowl of ice. Beat in the fromage blanc, a little at a time. Season well. Leave the mixture in the ice until required.

○ Season the salmon fillets with salt and pepper, then spread a quarter of the mousseline over each one.

○ Place the shallots and fish stock in a gratin dish, and arrange the salmon fillets in the stock, mousseline side up.

○ Cover and poach gently for 5–7 minutes. Remove from the stock, and keep warm.

○ Reduce the stock by half by boiling rapidly. Strain and spoon around the fish on individual serving plates.

SALMON SUPREME WITH BLACK NOODLES

Suprême de saumon d'Ecosse aux nouilles noires

The very unusual black noodles in this recipe – made with squid ink –
accompany the salmon perfectly.

4 PEOPLE

4	fillets of salmon, about 150g (5 oz) each, boned and skinned
4	sprigs of basil
75g (3 oz)	filo paste (approximately 4 sheets, see page 38)
20g (¾ oz)	shallots, finely chopped
10ml (2 tsp)	finely chopped garlic
200g (7 oz)	ripe tomatoes, skinned, seeded and diced
15ml (1 tbsp)	cut chives
1	quantity black noodles (see page 72)
	salt and finely ground pepper

○ Season the salmon fillets with salt and pepper, and place a sprig of basil on top of each.

○ Dip each sheet of filo paste momentarily in boiling water, and then in cold water. Remove immediately.

○ Wrap each salmon fillet in a blanched filo sheet.

○ Steam fillets for 3–4 minutes.

○ Sauté the shallots and garlic in a non-stick pan, stirring constantly, until transparent.

○ Add the tomatoes and sauté for about 1 minute.

○ Add the cut chives and season with salt and pepper.

○ Cook the black noodles in boiling salted water for about 3 minutes until *al dente*.

○ Drain the noodles, reserving 30ml (2 tbsp) cooking water, and rinse quickly in cold water. Toss the noodles with the reserved water in a saucepan over gentle heat, then season with salt and pepper.

○ Put the noodles on four individual plates and arrange the salmon on top. Make a small cut in the top of the pastry and gently ease out one of the basil leaves from the sprig. Garnish with the well-seasoned tomatoes (see photograph opposite page 104).

FILLET OF HALIBUT WITH TWO SAUCES

Fillet de flétan aux deux sauces

Vegetable sauces marry happily with fish, as they are natural in flavour, do
not overpower the flavour of the fish itself, and look good.

4 PEOPLE

4	fillets of halibut, about 150g (5 oz) each, skinned and boned
2	large yellow peppers
2	large red peppers
25g (1 oz)	shallots, finely chopped
2	small cloves of garlic, skinned and crushed
	a few sprigs of thyme
600ml (1¼ pt)	fish stock (see page 31), plus about 400ml (14 fl. oz) for steaming
	salt and freshly ground pepper

○ Wash and trim the peppers and cut into large pieces.

○ Sweat the shallots and garlic in a non-stick frying pan over a gentle heat without browning.

○ Divide the shallot mixture between two saucepans.

○ Add the yellow peppers to one pan and the red peppers to the other.

○ Divide the thyme and the 600ml (1¼ pt) fish stock between the two pans. Cover and simmer for 15 minutes until tender.

○ Liquidize each mixture until smooth, sieve if wished, then season to taste with salt and pepper.

○ Season the fish with salt and pepper and steam over the remaining 400ml (14 fl. oz) fish stock for 4–5 minutes.

○ Arrange the two well-seasoned hot sauces carefully on the plates (see the photograph opposite page 105). Top with the fish and serve at once.

GRILLED MONKFISH TAILS WITH FRESH HERBS

Queues de lotte grillées aux herbes

Monkfish used to be undervalued and cheap, but has now gained the recognition it deserves because of its good firm texture. It can be prepared in a variety of ways.

4 PEOPLE

4	small monkfish tails, about 225g (8 oz) each with bone
	juice of $\frac{1}{2}$ lemon
15g ($\frac{1}{2}$ oz)	freshly chopped and cut mixed herbs (such as dill, basil, thyme, marjoram)
1	small clove of garlic, skinned and crushed
	salt and freshly ground pepper
	parsley sprigs and lemon wedges to garnish

○ Carefully remove any skin from the fish tails, and trim well.

○ Sprinkle the fish with lemon juice, herbs and garlic, and leave to absorb the flavours for about an hour.

○ Remove the fish from the marinade, season with salt and pepper, and grill on both sides for about 8–10 minutes, turning once.

○ Arrange on a serving dish and garnish with parsley and lemon.

○ Serve, if liked, with tomato concasse (page 37).

MONKFISH RAGOUT WITH TOMATOES

Ragoût de lotte sans nom

4 PEOPLE

600g (1 lb, 5 oz)	fillets of monkfish
	juice of 1 lemon
1	small clove of garlic, skinned and crushed
1	sprig *each* of dill and rosemary, cut and chopped
6	basil leaves, finely cut
30ml (3 tbsp)	chopped parsley
2	onions, peeled and finely sliced
225g (8 oz)	yellow or red peppers, thinly sliced
100g (4 oz)	button mushrooms, thinly sliced
400g (14 oz)	tomatoes, skinned, seeded and diced
300ml ($\frac{1}{2}$ pt)	fish stock (see page 31)
	salt and freshly ground pepper

○ Remove any skin from the monkfish, discard, and cut flesh into 50g (2 oz) pieces.

○ Marinate the monkfish in the lemon juice with the garlic, herbs and salt and pepper for 1–2 hours.

○ Carefully sauté the onions and peppers in a large non-stick frying pan until just softened.

○ Add the mushrooms and cook for 1 minute, stirring.

○ Add the tomatoes and fish stock and bring to a simmer.

○ Add the drained fish pieces, cover and simmer for 6–8 minutes.

○ Remove the fish and vegetables from the pan and arrange on a suitable dish.

○ Boil the remaining stock rapidly until reduced by half. Pour over the fish and serve immediately.

STEAMED SARDINES
WITH FRESH CORIANDER LEAVES
Délice de sardines à la vapeur

Sardines – young pilchards – are now commonly available other than in cans, and steamed in this fashion, as opposed to grilling or baking, are quite delicious.

4 PEOPLE

8	sardines, cleaned and scales removed
20ml (4 tsp)	lemon juice
5ml (1 tsp)	sugar
20ml (4 tsp)	soya sauce
15g ($\frac{1}{2}$ oz)	fresh ginger root, peeled and cut into fine julienne strips
	freshly ground pepper
	fresh coriander leaves to garnish

○ Season the sardines with pepper and steam for 4–5 minutes.

○ Place the lemon juice, sugar, soya sauce and ginger julienne in a saucepan and bring to a simmer.

○ Arrange the sardines on individual plates, spoon a little sauce over each fish and garnish with coriander leaves.

FILLETS OF HERRING
WITH TOMATOES AND MUSTARD
Filets de hareng aux tomates et moutarde

Herring is becoming more popular again – like sardines – and, prepared
this way, is not only good for your health, but also tastes delicious.

4 PEOPLE

4	herrings, about 200g (7 oz) each
10ml (1 tsp)	herb mustard
150g (5 oz)	ripe tomatoes
	some fresh thyme leaves
25g (1 oz)	shallots, finely chopped
50ml (2 fl. oz)	fish stock (see page 31)
	salt and freshly ground pepper
	some fresh tarragon for garnish

○ Gut the herrings, cut off the fins and carefully remove the bone from the head downwards. Cut off heads. Remove the skin and take out remaining bones.

○ Wash the fillets and dry well. Season with salt and pepper, and rub the mustard on the inside of each fillet. Leave aside in a cool place for about 30 minutes.

○ Skin the tomatoes, quarter them and remove the core and seeds. Cut the flesh into 1cm ($\frac{1}{2}$ in) cubes.

○ Place the herring fillets in a non-stick frying pan, sprinkle with thyme leaves, and sauté on both sides until golden brown, about 2 minutes on each side. Remove and keep warm.

○ Sauté the shallots in the same pan until soft, then add the tomatoes and stock. Season, and heat gently.

○ Divide the tomato mixture between four warm plates and arrange the herring fillets on top. Garnish with fresh tarragon and serve immediately.

GRILLED FILLET OF TURBOT WITH CRAB

Médaillons de turbot, rêve du pêcheur

4 PEOPLE

4	fillets of turbot, about 150g (5 oz) each, skinned
25g (1 oz)	shallots, finely chopped
30ml (2 tbsp)	fresh wholewheat breadcrumbs
50g (2 oz)	white crab meat
10ml (2 tsp)	freshly cut dill
	a little fish stock (see page 31)
2	medium courgettes, finely diced
3	tomatoes, seeded and diced
	salt and freshly ground pepper

○ Season the fillets of turbot, then grill for 2 minutes on each side.

○ Sauté the shallots in a non-stick pan, stirring, until transparent.

○ Add the breadcrumbs, crab meat and dill, and moisten with a little fish stock.

○ Place this mixture on top of the turbot fillets and grill for about 5 minutes longer until the mixture is golden brown.

○ Blanch the courgettes in boiling salted water, drain and mix with the tomato dice.

○ Arrange the fish on four individual plates, and serve with the vegetables.

GOUJONS OF TURBOT WITH BASIL

Goujons de faisan de mer au basilic

4 PEOPLE

600g (1 lb, 5 oz)	fillet of turbot, skinned and boned, cut into strips about 15g (½ oz) each
2.5ml (½ tsp)	finely chopped orange peel, blanched
150ml (¼ pt)	fish stock (see page 31)
20g (¾ oz)	shallots, finely chopped
80g (3¼ oz)	turnips, peeled, cut into strips and blanched
8	basil leaves, cut into fine julienne strips
12	orange segments
	salt and finely ground pepper

○ Season the fillets with salt, pepper and orange peel.

○ Put the fish stock and shallots in a suitable casserole.

○ Add the goujons of turbot, cover and poach carefully for about 2 minutes.

○ Remove the fish and keep warm. Reduce the stock by one-third.

○ Add the turnips and basil to the stock and season to taste. Simmer for about 30 seconds – the turnips should still be crunchy.

○ Take a little stock out, and in it gently warm through the orange segments in a separate pan.

○ Place the goujons of turbot in a suitable dish with the turnips and basil, and cover with the well-seasoned stock.

○ Garnish with the warm orange segments.

FILLETS OF SOLE
WITH GRAPES AND WALNUTS

Délices de sole aux raisins et noix

Extra whole cooked crayfish (body shell removed) can be used as a garnish
as well as the parsley.

4 PEOPLE

8	fillets of sole, about 75g (3 oz) each
4	scallops, cut in half
4	scampi, shells removed, cut in half
4	crayfish, cooked for 2 minutes and shells removed
20	white Muscat grapes, peeled and pips removed
12	halves of sweet walnuts, blanched, peeled and cut in half
	juice of $\frac{1}{2}$ lemon
100ml (4 fl. oz)	brown veal stock (see page 26)
5ml (1 tsp)	finely chopped parsley
	salt and freshly ground pepper

○ Season the fillets of sole with salt and pepper.

○ Sauté in a non-stick pan for 2–3 minutes on each side. Keep warm.

○ Sauté the seasoned scallops, scampi and crayfish for 30 seconds. Add the grapes and walnut halves.

○ Place the fillets of sole on a suitable dish, and arrange the sautéed seafood, grapes and walnuts on top.

○ Add the lemon juice to the hot veal stock, mix in well, then pour carefully around the fillets of sole.

○ Garnish decoratively with chopped parsley.

FILLETS OF JOHN DORY
WITH TOMATO SAUCE
Filets de St Pierre à la sauce pommes d'amour

As the tomatoes in the sauce are only heated, not cooked, they retain their
vitamins fully.

4 PEOPLE

2	John Dory fish, weighing about 1.5kg (3–3½ lb) in total
	salt and freshly ground pepper

Tomato sauce

400g (14 oz)	firm, ripe tomatoes, blanched and skinned
20ml (4 tsp)	reduced vegetable stock (see page 30)
5ml (1 tsp)	Dijon mustard
1	small clove of garlic, peeled and crushed
5ml (1 tsp)	*each* of chopped parsley, and finely cut tarragon, coriander leaves and chervil
8	coriander leaves
	salt and freshly ground pepper

○ To make the sauce, halve the tomatoes crosswise, remove the seeds and chop the flesh into tiny dice.

○ Mix together the reduced stock, mustard, garlic and herbs. Stir in the tomato dice and season to taste with salt and pepper.

○ Wash the fish thoroughly and, using a filleting knife, carefully remove the fillets.

○ Skin the fillets and trim well.

○ Season with salt and pepper, then steam for 3–4 minutes.

○ Heat the sauce very gently in a bowl over hot water.

○ Put the slightly warm sauce on four individual plates. Arrange the fillets of fish on top and serve immediately. Garnish with coriander leaves.

Salmon Suprème with Black Noodles (see page 95)

Fillet of Turbot with Yellow Pepper Sauce and Basil (see page 101)

Steamed Red Mullet Fillet with Vegetables, here prepared as an hors d'oeuvre (see page 67)

Fillet of Halibut with Two Sauces (see page 96)

STEWED EELS WITH GARLIC
Anguilles à l'ail

4 PEOPLE

675g (1½ lb)	fresh eel, skinned
25g (1 oz)	shallots, finely chopped
1	clove of garlic, skinned and crushed
350ml (12 fl. oz)	fish stock (see page 31)
1	bouquet garni (leek, celery, thyme, parsley stalks and onion, tied together)
12	button onions
100g (4 oz)	tomatoes, skinned, seeded and diced
8	button mushrooms, well washed and dried
30ml (2 tbsp)	chopped parsley
	squeeze of lemon juice
	salt and freshly ground pepper

○ Cut the skinned eel into bite-sized pieces.

○ Sweat the shallots in a non-stick pan without browning for about 2 minutes.

○ Add the pieces of eel and sweat for a further 2 minutes, then add the garlic.

○ Add the fish stock, bouquet garni and button onions. Cover and simmer for 7–8 minutes.

○ Add the tomatoes, mushrooms and parsley. Simmer for 1–2 minutes.

○ Remove bouquet garni. Season to taste with lemon juice, salt and pepper. Serve immediately.

SHELLFISH

Shellfish are divided into many groups. For example, there are bivalve molluscs, which are invertebrates with a hinged shell (mussels, oysters and scallops). Crustaceans have a protective external skeleton, a jointed 'shell' (lobsters, crabs, prawns, etc.). Like fish in general, and white fish in particular, shellfish of all varieties are packed with protein, vitamins and minerals and are low in fat. Shellfish are used a lot in Cuisine Naturelle recipes, many having already appeared in the Soups and Hors d'Oeuvres chapters. Shellfish are best if prepared as simply as possible, are light, nutritious, delicious to eat, and ideal for Cuisine Naturelle cooking.

Remember to try a little fish herb mixture (see page 40) instead of some of the salt content in the following recipes.

Crayfish *Écrevisse*

A small, freshwater crustacean. The best are those with red legs, which are larger and come mostly from Turkey and Poland. They should always be cooked live, in boiling court bouillon. It is common practice to de-vein crayfish before cooking, and essential for the flavour. Please note:

1. The cooking liquid should always be ready and boiling.
2. Work in small batches.
3. Hold the crayfish by the carapace, twist the middle section of the end of the tail by pulling carefully, then draw out the fragile blue thread.
4. Cook the crayfish immediately.

Lobster *Homard*

One of the largest crustaceans, and the best in flavour are the female lobsters from the coasts of Brittany, Ireland and Scotland (males are less tasty because they run too much, do not feed properly, and exhaust themselves with their love affairs!). Not only does the female have a delicate strip of meat in the head, lacking in the male, but when pregnant has the tasty eggs or coral under the tail (a female lobster can be identified by the wider shell underneath, to accommodate the eggs). Lobster eggs should always be kept, cooked separately, and used for garnish. The ideal weight is 800–900g (1¾–2 lb). Lobsters should be cooked live; always choose one that is lively, heavy for its size, with a hard shell. The tail should spring back when straightened out.

Mussels *Moules*

A familiar bivalve which is found around the world's coasts, and is rich in minerals like iron and iodine - required by the body in small amounts, but essential for health. If you collect your own, always make sure that the water is unpolluted; if buying, discard any with broken shells or which are open and do not close immediately when tapped. To clean thoroughly before cooking, place in clean water with a little salt for a couple of hours. Before cooking, the shells must be scraped, scrubbed and well washed to get rid of sand. Always cooked live, any which have not opened after a few minutes' cooking should be discarded.

Oysters *Huîtres*

The biggest are by no means the best, and a variety of sizes and shapes come from all over the world - the best known from France, Portugal, the Mediterranean, the American Atlantic coast, and, from the Essex and Kentish beds of Britain, the 'natives'.

The best are considered to be Belons from the river of the same name in Finistère. Oysters for eating raw, and for cooking, should be alive and fresh; for eating raw, they should really be opened a maximum of 15 minutes before.

Prawns and Shrimps *Crevettes*

Small crustaceans which come in a multitude of colours and sizes. The smallest in Britain are brown or pink and soft shelled, and are usually sold cooked; the larger varieties available - Dublin Bay prawns and Pacific prawns - more closely resemble lobster, with a hard shell. Scampi or langoustine are other names for the Norway lobster or Dublin Bay prawn.

Scallops *Coquilles St-Jacques*

These are bivalves, and there are many species in many seas: for example queens, pétoncles or bay scallops. After leaving the water, scallops live for about 30–36 hours. Many can be bought opened and cleaned in the half shell, but I would recommend buying only those that are still closed. Scrub well, as with other bivalves, and open with a strong knife before heating on a hot-plate or in a hot pan in order to open them fully.

To prepare, with a soup spoon remove the white flesh (the 'noix') from the brown frill (the eyes, gills and mantle). Wash briefly, then separate the coral from the noix and squeeze the coral to remove any black liquid. Carefully remove any traces of the silvery-white tendon, which is very tough. Use scallops and coral as soon as possible.

MARINATED SCALLOPS SUSAN HAMPSHIRE

Noix de coquilles St-Jacques, Susan Hampshire

This dish – created especially for my good friend Susan Hampshire – relies very much on the visual effect of the mounds of vegetables surrounding the scallops. The vegetables must all be cut into *very* fine julienne strips.

4 PEOPLE

12	fresh scallops in their shells
	juice of 1 lime
15g ($\frac{1}{2}$ oz)	fresh ginger root, peeled and cut into very fine julienne strips
15g ($\frac{1}{2}$ oz)	fresh coriander leaves, finely cut
100g (4 oz)	carrots, peeled
100g (4 oz)	celery, trimmed
100g (4 oz)	courgettes, topped and tailed
100g (4 oz)	red pepper, cored and seeded
50g (2 oz)	mangetout, topped and tailed
50g (2 oz)	radish, topped and tailed
150g (5 oz)	low-fat natural yoghurt
20g ($\frac{3}{4}$ oz)	lobster eggs (optional)
	salt and freshly ground pepper

○ Open the scallops with the tip of a small strong knife, then scoop the scallops off the half shell with a soup spoon. Remove the debris and wash briefly but thoroughly to remove all the grit. Remove the orange coral.

○ Cut the scallops horizontally into circles with a sharp knife.

○ Lay the scallops on a plate and sprinkle with lime juice, ginger and cut coriander. Season with salt and pepper and leave to marinate for 5 minutes.

○ Meanwhile, cut each vegetable separately into fine julienne strips. Add a little yoghurt to each vegetable mound, season well and mix in thoroughly.

○ If using them, place lobster eggs in a saucepan with a minimum of water, 5ml (1 tsp) vinegar, and a pinch of salt. Bring to the boil, drain and cool quickly in iced water.

○ Place marinated scallop slices in the centre of each of four individual plates. Decorate the outside of each plate with mounds of the different vegetables and the lobster eggs. Serve immediately.

SCALLOPS WITH TOMATOES AND BASIL

Coquilles St-Jacques aux tomates et basilic

4 PEOPLE

16	large scallops in their shells
15ml (1 tbsp)	finely chopped shallots
300ml ($\frac{1}{2}$ pt)	fish stock (see page 31)
	a pinch of saffron strands
200g (1 oz)	fromage blanc (see page 33)
3	large tomatoes, skinned, seeded and diced
15ml (1 tbsp)	basil, cut into very fine julienne strips
	salt and freshly ground pepper
8	basil leaves to garnish

○ Open the scallops with a sharp knife and lay on a warm hot-plate (or in a hot pan) for a few minutes until they open completely. Remove the scallops and coral with a soup spoon. Carefully separate the scallops from the coral and wash briefly but thoroughly.

○ Halve the scallops and lay on a cloth to dry.

○ Sweat the finely chopped shallots in a non-stick pan without letting them brown.

○ Pour in the fish stock and allow to simmer for 2 minutes. Add the coral and simmer for 15 seconds, then add the scallops and simmer for a further 15 seconds.

○ Remove the scallops and coral from the stock and keep them warm.

○ Bring the stock to the boil, add the saffron and simmer for 5 minutes. Stir in the fromage blanc, and warm gently without boiling.

○ Add two-thirds of the tomatoes with the cut basil and season to taste.

○ Spoon the sauce on to four individual plates, and arrange the scallops and coral on top. Garnish with the reserved tomato dice and the basil leaves.

CASSEROLE OF MUSSELS WITH FENNEL

Cassolette de moules parfumées au fenouil

This is a very honest way of producing a mussel recipe. Mussels taste very good with the fennel, but you could also use curry spices, saffron or other flavourings.

4 PEOPLE

2kg (4½ lb)	mussels, scrubbed, brushed and beard removed
550ml (1 pt)	water
15g (½ oz)	shallot, finely chopped
15g (½ oz)	celery, diced
100g (4 oz)	fennel, finely cut
	a few parsley stalks
	a little thyme
30g (1¼ oz)	*each* of leek and carrot, cut into fine julienne strips
	salt, freshly ground pepper and Cayenne
8	fennel leaves for garnish

○ Discard any mussels that float during the cleaning, or that refuse to close when tapped sharply with a knife. Wash thoroughly.

○ Bring the water, shallot, celery, half the fennel, the parsley and thyme to the boil in a wide, shallow pan.

○ Add the mussels in one layer, season with pepper, cover and bring to the boil again. Boil only until the mussels open – about 3–4 minutes – or else they will become tough. Discard any that have not opened.

○ Remove the mussels from the stock with a sieve or skimming ladle. Strain the stock carefully through fine cloth (to get rid of any sand), and then reduce by boiling to about 200ml (7 fl. oz).

○ Meanwhile, take the mussels out of their shells, remove and discard any remaining beards and dark 'elastic bands', and keep the mussels warm.

○ Sauté the rest of the fennel with the carrot and leek julienne in a non-stick pan for about 2 minutes, stirring constantly.

○ Add the vegetables and shelled mussels to the reduced hot stock, and season to taste.

○ Serve in individual bowls or soup plates, and garnish with fennel leaves.

POACHED OYSTERS
WRAPPED IN LETTUCE LEAVES

Huîtres en feuilles vertes

Oysters – renowned more for their supposed aphrodisiac properties than
for their protein content – are wrapped in lettuce leaves for an unusual and
attractive dish.

4 PEOPLE

24	small lettuce leaves
24	oysters
15g (½ oz)	shallots, finely chopped
225ml (8 fl. oz)	fish stock (see page 31)
15g (½ oz)	*each* of carrot, leek and celery,
	washed, trimmed, peeled and cut
	into fine julienne strips
	a squeeze of lemon juice
	salt and freshly ground pepper

○ Plunge the lettuce leaves into boiling water. Return to the boil then remove at once to ice-cold water. Drain well and remove any coarse stems.

○ Open the oysters with an oyster knife or small strong knife. Strain the liquid into the fish stock and reserve.

○ Remove oysters from the shells and cut away the tendon. Season with pepper.

○ Wrap each oyster in a lettuce leaf. Reserve and wash shells, and warm them.

○ Gently sauté the shallots without colouring in a non-stick pan.

○ Add the fish stock, with the oyster water, and heat to a gentle simmer. Add the oyster packages and poach for 15 seconds. Remove the oysters and keep warm.

○ Boil stock rapidly for 3–4 minutes until reduced by half.

○ Add the carrot, leek and celery julienne and cook for 1 minute. Season to taste with lemon juice, salt and pepper.

○ Place an oyster package back in each shell and spoon the sauce over. Serve at once.

Scallops with Tomatoes and Basil (see page 110)

Crayfish Ragoût with Green Asparagus (see page 115)

PRAWNS WITH COURGETTES AND GINGER

Crevettes aux courgettes et gingembre

4 PEOPLE

12	large raw prawns, peeled (reserve shells for stock)
50g (2 oz)	spring onions, trimmed and sliced
5ml (1 tsp)	chopped fresh ginger root
150g (5 oz)	courgettes, thinly sliced
50g (2 oz)	red pepper, cored, skinned and thinly sliced
15ml (1 tbsp)	chopped parsley
	a squeeze of lemon juice
	salt and Cayenne pepper
	dill sprigs to garnish

Prawn stock

15g ($\frac{1}{2}$ oz)	shallots, finely chopped
$\frac{1}{2}$	clove of garlic, skinned and chopped
	a few sprigs of parsley
225ml (8 fl. oz)	water
	salt and freshly ground pepper

○ Make the prawn stock by sautéing the prawn shells in a non-stick pan for 2 minutes. Add the shallots, garlic and parsley and sauté for a further 5 minutes.

○ Add the water and bring to the boil, then cover and simmer for 20 minutes. Pass through fine muslin, then season to taste.

○ Start the remainder of the recipe by sautéing the spring onions and ginger in a non-stick pan without browning.

○ Add the courgettes and sauté for 1 minute before adding 150ml ($\frac{1}{4}$ pt) of the prawn stock.

○ Add the pepper slices and simmer gently for about 2–3 minutes until the stock is reduced slightly.

○ Add the parsley and lemon juice and season to taste with salt and Cayenne.

○ Season the raw prawns with salt and pepper and poach in the remaining stock for 2–3 minutes. Remove, and add the stock to the vegetables.

○ Arrange the vegetable mixture on four individual plates. Place the prawns on top and garnish with dill sprigs.

GRILLED SEAFOOD SAUSAGES
WITH CARROT LEAF SAUCE

Boudins de fruits de mer, sauce aux feuilles de carottes

Sausage skins are now easily available, but if they are too firm, remove them carefully from the sausages before grilling – the poaching will have set the filling in shape. When carrot tops are not available for the sauce, use a mixture of green leaves and herbs such as watercress, sorrel and parsley. This can be served either as an hors d'oeuvre or a main course: halve quantities for the former; add a nice accompaniment for the latter.

4 PEOPLE

4	scallops in their shells
4	scampi, removed from shells, about 100g (4 oz) peeled weight
150g (5 oz)	fillet of salmon, skinned, boned and cut into small cubes
100g (4 oz)	fillet of monkfish, skinned and cut into small cubes
200g (7 oz)	fillet of whiting or pike, skinned and boned
1	egg white
100g (4 oz)	fromage blanc (see page 33)
30ml (2 tbsp)	finely cut dill
40-50cm (16–20 in)	sausage skin, soaked in water
	salt and freshly ground pepper

Sauce

300g (11 oz)	carrot tops without stalks, washed
200ml (7 fl. oz)	fish stock (see page 31)
300g (11 oz)	fromage blanc (see page 33)
	salt and freshly ground pepper

○ Open the scallops with a strong knife and place on the hot-plate (or in a hot pan) for a few minutes to open them completely, then remove from the shells with a soup spoon.

○ Separate the scallops carefully from the coral and debris, and wash quickly.

○ Cut the scallops and coral into small pieces and lay on a cloth to dry.

○ Season the scallops, scampi, salmon and monkfish with salt and pepper.

○ Purée the whiting or pike in a food processor. Add the egg white and a pinch of salt and pepper, and process until smooth.

○ Place the puréed fish mixture in a basin over ice. Gradually beat in fromage blanc.

○ Add all the seasoned fish and the chopped dill. Season, and leave to rest for 30–40 minutes. The consistency should be like a choux paste mixture.

- To make the sauce, retain four carrot sprigs for garnish, then blanch the remainder in the fish stock for about 1 minute. Drain, dip in cold water, then drain again.

- Purée the carrot tops in a liquidizer, adding some of the liquid if necessary. Strain.

- Reduce the remaining fish stock by half by rapid boiling.

- Add the fromage blanc and the purée to the reduced stock and mix until smooth. Bring to the boil and season.

- Fill the sausage skin with the fish mixture, using a piping bag or spoon and shape into four 'sausages' about 10cm (4 in) long. Bind the ends of each sausage with string.

- Poach them in hot water (do not boil) for about 5–6 minutes. Drain and cool in cold water. (The skin can now be removed if wished.)

- Grill under medium heat for 5–6 minutes, turning occasionally, until golden brown.

- Spoon the warm sauce on to four plates and place the 'sausages' on top. Garnish each plate with a small piece of carrot top.

CRAYFISH RAGOUT WITH GREEN ASPARAGUS

Ragoût d'écrevisses et d'asperges vertes

4 PEOPLE

36	live crayfish
16	green asparagus tips, peeled
12	very small new carrots, peeled and blanched
15ml (1 tbsp)	finely chopped shallots
300ml ($\frac{1}{2}$ pt)	crayfish stock (see below)
	salt and freshly ground pepper
4	sprigs of chervil to garnish

- Cook the crayfish in boiling salted water for 1 minute (see page 107). Remove from the water and place in a bowl of ice to cool quickly.

- Remove the tails from the shells and reserve body and tail shells to make stock (follow method for Prawn Stock in preceding recipe). Keep the tails fresh (cover with a damp cloth).

- Cook the asparagus in lightly salted water until just tender, about 3 minutes.

- Sauté the shallots gently, without browning, until transparent, stirring constantly.

- Add the crayfish stock and bring to the boil. Continue boiling until reduced by half.

- Strain into a clean saucepan, adjust seasoning, then add the crayfish, asparagus and carrots, and heat carefully without boiling.

- Arrange in individual soup plates and garnish with sprigs of chervil.

SYMPHONIE DE FRUITS DE MER

This can be served as either an hors d'oeuvre or a main course.

4 PEOPLE

4	large fresh scallops in their shells
12	fresh mussels in their shells
8	tiny squid
150g (5 oz)	fillet of turbot, skinned and cut into cubes about 15g ($\frac{1}{2}$ oz) each
12	scampi, removed from their shells
8	raw Mediterranean prawns, heads and shells removed
50g (2 oz)	leeks, white part mainly
400ml (14 fl. oz)	fish stock (see page 31)
4	sprigs of fresh thyme
	Cayenne, salt and freshly ground pepper

○ Open the scallops with a small, strong knife by easing the scallop flesh away from the debris and flat shell.

○ Wash briefly but thoroughly, then separate the coral from the scallops. Cut each scallop in half horizontally and lay on a damp cloth with the coral.

○ Scrub the mussel shells and remove the beard. Place in a saucepan and heat gently until the mussels open. Discard any that remain closed.

○ Remove the tentacles from the squid (reserve the bodies for another dish). Wash well and blanch in boiling water for 30 seconds. Drain and cool.

○ Season the turbot, scampi and prawns with Cayenne, salt and pepper.

○ Thinly slice the leeks and blanch in boiling salted water. Drain and cool.

○ Heat the fish stock to a gentle simmer, add the squid and prawns, and poach for 1 minute.

○ Add the scampi and turbot and poach for 1 minute.

○ Add the leeks, mussels and scallop coral and poach for a further 30 seconds.

○ Add the scallops and thyme and poach for yet another 30 seconds.

○ Carefully arrange the fish in four individual soup dishes.

○ Check the seasoning of the stock and adjust to taste. Bring just to serving temperature, then pour over the fish and serve at once.

LOBSTER WITH TOMATO AND WATERCRESS

Homard à la tomate et au cresson

With the technique outlined below, the lobster stays tender and moist,
whilst the sautéing gives extra flavour.

4 PEOPLE

4	live female lobsters, about 350g (12 oz) each
3 litres (5¼ pt)	court bouillon (see page 32)
8	basil leaves, finely cut
1	quantity of tomato coulis (see page 119)

Watercress purée

400g (14 oz)	watercress, *or* 225g (8 oz) prepared weight of watercress leaves
1.2 litres (good 2 pt)	water
	juice of ½ lemon
40g (1½ oz)	tofu
	salt and freshly ground pepper

○ Splash the live lobsters with cold water then plunge them into the boiling court bouillon for 2 minutes.

○ Remove the pan from the heat, but leave the lobsters in the court bouillon. Place the pan in a large bowl of ice to cool quickly.

○ Meanwhile make the watercress purée and the tomato coulis (for which see page 119).

○ For the purée, remove the larger stalks from the watercress, and blanch the leaves in the measured boiling salted water for about 1 minute.

○ Drain the watercress, then plunge immediately into iced water (this holds the colour and stops the cooking process). Drain again and dry on absorbent kitchen paper.

○ Purée in a liquidizer with the lemon juice and tofu.

○ Warm the sauce in a double-boiler, stirring occasionally. Check seasoning.

○ When the lobster is cold, remove the tails and cut through the shell underneath with scissors. Remove and carefully shell the claws, discarding the cartilage.

○ Cut the tail into medallions about 6mm (¼ in) thick, and cut the claws in half.

○ Place the lobster meat in a hot non-stick pan and add the sliced basil leaves. Sauté for 5 seconds on each side.

○ Pour the tomato coulis on to four individual plates. Arrange the lobster medallions, claw meat and basil on top and spoon a little warm watercress purée over them.

SAUTEED SCALLOPS WITH LEEK PUREE
Coquilles St-Jacques à la purée de poireaux

4 PEOPLE

8	large fresh scallops in their shells
300g (11 oz)	tender green of leeks, trimmed
75ml (3 fl. oz)	fish stock (see page 31)
50g (2 oz)	fromage blanc (see page 33)
	salt and freshly ground pepper
4	fresh basil leaves to garnish

○ Open the scallops by inserting the tip of a small strong knife between the two half shells to ease them apart. Remove the scallop with a soup spoon.

○ Clean very well, removing the debris and coral (reserve the latter for garnish), then wash briefly and dry thoroughly.

○ Cut the leeks into pieces and wash very well.

○ Cook the leeks in the stock until tender, about 5 minutes. Liquidize, then stir in the fromage blanc and season to taste.

○ Cut the scallops in half, and sauté halves and coral in a non-stick pan. The coral needs about 10 seconds each side, the scallop halves about 5 seconds on each side.

○ Spoon the leek purée on to individual plates. Arrange the scallops on top, then garnish each plate with some coral and a basil leaf.

GLAZED OYSTERS ON A BED OF CRAB
Huîtres et crabe des isles gratinées

4 PEOPLE

24	oysters
	juice of $\frac{1}{2}$ lemon
60ml (4 tbsp)	fish stock (see page 31)
1	egg yolk
75g (3 oz)	white crab meat
	salt and freshly ground pepper
	lemon crown and tomato rose to garnish

- Open the oysters and cut away the silver tendon that holds the oyster to the shell. Remove the oysters from their shells. Strain any liquid into a small pan.
- Place oysters in the pan with the lemon juice and stock, and poach for 15 seconds.
- Remove from the pan, and reduce the stock by half by rapid boiling.
- Remove from heat and whisk in egg yolk. Season to taste with a little salt and pepper.
- Wash the bottom half of each oyster shell and place a little warmed crab meat in each.
- Place the oysters on top and coat with the sauce. Place under a hot grill for about 30 seconds until golden.
- Serve at once on a dish garnished with a lemon crown and tomato rose.

TOMATO COULIS

Sauce coulis de tomates

This is a pure sauce, colourful and tasty, which can be used for many other Cuisine Naturelle recipes. Finely chopped tomatoes can be added to the sauce as a garnish before use.

4 PEOPLE

550g (1¼ lb)	firm, ripe tomatoes, skinned and seeded
40g (1½ oz)	shallots, finely chopped
½	clove of garlic, skinned and crushed
2	sprigs of fresh thyme
2	sprigs of fresh rosemary
50ml (2 fl. oz)	reduced vegetable stock (see page 30)
	salt and freshly ground pepper

- Make sure all seeds, skin and excess juice have been eliminated from the tomatoes.
- Sauté the shallots and garlic in a non-stick pan for 3–4 minutes, stirring constantly.
- Add the herbs and sauté for about 1 minute, very gently.
- Add the tomatoes and vegetable stock and simmer for 10–12 minutes.
- Remove the herbs and purée the sauce in a blender.
- Put the sauce back into the saucepan, bring to the boil, and season with salt and pepper.

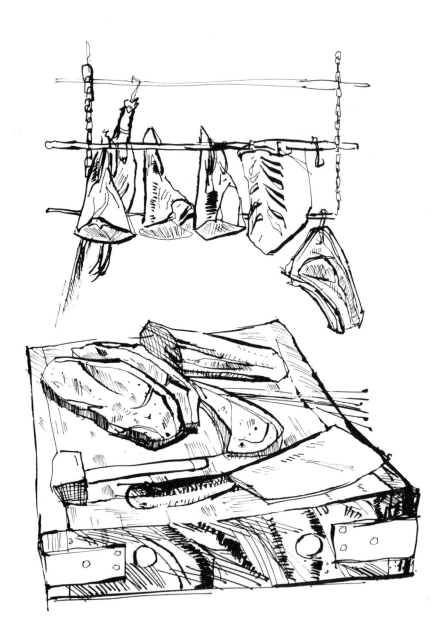

MEAT

Meat is full of protein, but also contains hidden fat. It is, of course, this hidden fat that moistens the meat, and gives it its flavour - and Cuisine Naturelle would not wish to deny anyone the undoubted pleasures of a good, tender slice of meat. The Cuisine Naturelle solution is, as in all the other recipes, to prepare without butter, cream or oil - any *added* fat - and alcohol. The meats selected are the leanest possible, all obvious fat is cut away carefully, and the chosen sauces and accompaniments are natural, complementing, flavouring and moistening. The quantity of meat served has been reduced as well, to create a better balance - people are tending to eat less meat these days anyway.

Good meat needs to be cut carefully, not haphazardly. Connective tissues lying between the muscles make it easier to separate the various parts, thus subcutaneous layers of fat and sinews can be removed without much difficulty, leaving the compact muscles. The most tender meat comes from the parts of the animals that have 'moved' least, the muscles being tougher at leg, neck and shoulder.

Meat should always be kept dry, away from steam and products that produce steam, as it becomes 'sticky' with damp.

Meat offal - liver, kidney, sweetbreads and tongue - are usually the healthiest parts of the animal to eat. They are comparatively low in fat, and most contain a high proportion of vitamins and minerals - liver, for instance, is rich in Vitamins A and B, and iron.

To cut down on the use of salt in the following recipes, use some of the herb mixture for meat on page 40.

Beef *Boeuf*

Young first-class beef should be red in colour, but not too dark. A marbled effect on the meat - of fat running through the tissue - is a sign of proper fattening, and of the breed of the animal, and will guarantee its tenderness. Beef should be hung for about 15 to 21 days before use.

Veal *Veau*

A properly fattened, milk-fed, calf will have a pinkish-white flesh, and the kidney should be completely covered in white fat. Meat from calves that are too young, or that have not been fattened properly, will disintegrate during preparation. Veal should be hung for 8 to 10 days before use.

Lamb *Agneau*

Most chefs prefer lamb to beef and pork because it is more tender, with a pronounced taste of its own. Lamb should always be prepared as simply as possible to preserve that special taste. The best meat comes from grazing sheep that are not yet fully grown - about ten months old. Milk-fed lambs - only available in spring - are animals that are still suckling and not yet grazing; they have white flesh. Lamb, like all other kinds of meat, should be hung for a few days before use.

Pork *Porc*

Good pork is pale pink in colour and slightly marbled. It should never be dark red or watery. It should be hung for 5 to 6 days before use.

BEEF SIRLOIN, DANNY KAYE

Entrecôte double de boeuf, Danny Kaye

This recipe was first prepared for Danny Kaye, who is not only a world-famous actor, but is also an extremely good cook. Some of my happiest hours have been spent in his company.
Serve the almost raw beef slices with Meaux mustard or a mustard sauce handed separately.

4 PEOPLE

675g (1½ lb)	beef sirloin steak in one piece, boned and well trimmed of fat
30ml (2 tbsp)	black peppercorns, crushed
15ml (1 tbsp)	red wine vinegar
5ml (1 tsp)	soya sauce
5ml (1 tsp)	*each* of chopped shallot and finely cut chives
2.5ml (½ tsp)	*each* of chopped tarragon, and finely cut parsley and garlic
3	egg whites
	salt and freshly ground pepper
	watercress leaves to garnish

○ Rub the sirloin with peppercorns and salt.

○ In a non-stick frying pan – or directly on a hot-plate – brown and seal the sirloin, about 2 minutes on each side.

○ Whisk together the vinegar, soya sauce, shallot, chives, tarragon, parsley and garlic until thick. Season to taste.

○ Whisk egg whites until frothy, then add dressing and whisk again.

○ Thinly slice the steak, arrange on a plate or on individual plates, and spoon the dressing over. Serve immediately, garnished with watercress.

FILLET OF BEEF
WITH ROSEMARY AND MUSTARD
Rosette de boeuf gratiné au romarin

Garnish the steaks with vegetables of choice. In the photograph opposite
page 129 we have used leaf spinach with toasted croûtons, new carrots and
Jacqueline potatoes.

4 PEOPLE

4	fillet steaks, about 150g (5 oz) each, well trimmed of fat
20g ($\frac{3}{4}$ oz)	shallots, finely chopped
5ml (1 tsp)	finely chopped garlic
400ml (14 fl. oz)	brown veal stock (see page 26)
75g (3 oz)	fresh breadcrumbs
10ml (2 tsp)	freshly chopped parsley
10ml (2 tsp)	freshly chopped rosemary
	juice of $\frac{1}{2}$ lemon
10ml (2 tsp)	English mustard
	salt and freshly ground pepper

○ Season the fillets with salt and pepper.

○ Sauté in a hot non-stick pan for about 2 minutes on each side. Remove from the pan and keep warm.

○ Add the shallots and garlic to the pan, and sauté at a lower temperature, stirring constantly, until transparent.

○ Add the brown veal stock and reduce by half by rapid boiling.

○ In the meantime, mix the breadcrumbs and herbs together. Add the lemon juice.

○ Brush the mustard on top of each fillet.

○ Top with the herb mixture and put the fillets under a hot grill until golden brown (about 1–2 minutes).

○ Put the well-seasoned sauce and meat on a plate and garnish with vegetables of choice.

MIGNONS OF BEEF WITH SHALLOT SAUCE

Mignons de boeuf sautés aux échalotes

Filet mignon is also known as fillet steak, and is a small cut from the fillet. It
is lean and tender, and should be handled with great love and care.

4 PEOPLE

8	mignons of beef, well trimmed, about 65g (2½ oz) each
40g (1½ oz)	shallots, finely chopped
300ml (½ pt)	brown veal stock (see page 26)
5ml (1 tsp)	lemon juice
	salt and freshly ground pepper

○ Season the well-trimmed mignons with salt and pepper.

○ Sauté them on both sides in a hot non-stick pan for 3–4 minutes altogether. Remove
the mignons and keep warm.

○ Add the chopped shallots to the pan and sauté gently without browning.

○ Add the brown veal stock and reduce by rapid boiling to half its original volume.

○ Season with salt, pepper and lemon juice.

○ Coat the mignons with the sauce and serve immediately.

GRILLED RIB OF BEEF WITH GARDEN HERBS

Côte de boeuf grillée aux herbes du jardin

To prevent the meat juices from escaping, the beef should rest for
10 minutes before being cut. Serve with Carrot and Spinach Mousse
(see page 165).
The wing rib, closest to the sirloin, is recommended for this recipe.

4 PEOPLE

1.2kg (2½ lb)	piece of beef rib, with bone, and trimmed well of fat
1	small sprig of thyme
1	small sprig of rosemary
4	sage leaves, finely cut
1	clove of garlic, crushed
	salt and coarsely ground black pepper
1	bunch of watercress, well washed and trimmed, for garnish

○ Using a rolling pin or a meat mallet, flatten the beef to the depth of the rib bone.

○ Place in a shallow dish.

○ Finely chop all the herbs and mix with the garlic.

○ Press the herbs on to both sides of the meat and leave, covered in a cool place, for 2–3 hours.

○ Season with salt and pepper.

○ Grill under medium heat for 10–12 minutes, turning once during this time.

○ Serve in slices garnished with watercress sprigs.

LOIN OF LAMB
WITH THYME AND SPINACH

Longe d'agneau au thym et épinards

A mousse of broccoli may be served if tender young spinach is not available.

4 PEOPLE

2	loins of lamb, about 550g (1¼ lb) weight, after boning and trimming well of fat
30g (1¼ oz)	shallots, finely chopped
1	clove of garlic, finely chopped
15g (½ oz)	fresh thyme sprigs
400ml (14 fl. oz)	lamb stock (see page 27)
350g (12 oz)	fresh spinach leaves, stalks removed, roughly chopped, blanched and well drained
50g (2 oz)	fromage blanc (see page 33)
	salt and freshly ground pepper
4	small tomatoes, skinned and seeded, then each cut into 4 diamond shapes, for garnish
16	tiny sprigs of thyme for garnish

○ Season the lamb loins with salt and pepper, then sauté them in a non-stick pan for about 6–7 minutes, turning once. Remove from the pan and keep warm.

○ Add 20g (¾ oz) of the shallots, with the garlic and thyme, to the pan and sauté, stirring all the time, until the shallots are transparent.

○ Add the lamb stock and reduce, by boiling, to half the quantity. Strain and season to taste. Keep the sauce warm.

○ Sauté the remaining shallots in a non-stick pan.

○ Add the spinach leaves and sauté for about 2 minutes.

○ Add the fromage blanc, mix well and season to taste.

○ Press the spinach mixture into four small ramekin dishes and leave to set for 30 seconds.

○ Place a tiny sprig of thyme on to each tomato diamond and place in a low oven – about 150°C/300°F/Gas 2 – until warmed through.

○ Spoon a little sauce into the centre of each of four plates. Unmould the spinach domes on to the centre of each plate.

○ Slice each piece of lamb into eight pieces. Arrange four slices around each dome.

○ Garnish with the tomato diamonds and serve at once.

POACHED SADDLE OF LAMB

Selle d'agneau pochée à la paysanne

To give this dish a special taste, poach an unpeeled clove of garlic in the
stock along with the lamb and vegetables. As the garlic is uncrushed, the
flavour is much more subtle.

4 PEOPLE

600g (1 lb, 5 oz)	saddle of lamb, boned and well trimmed of fat
300ml ($\frac{1}{2}$ pt)	white veal stock (see page 24)
300ml ($\frac{1}{2}$ pt)	lamb stock (see page 27)
75g (3 oz)	*each* of white and red onions, peeled, quartered and broken up
150g (5 oz)	white of leek, cut into diagonal slices
150g (5 oz)	Savoy cabbage leaves, roughly chopped
100g (4 oz)	small Brussels sprouts, divided into individual leaves
	a little finely chopped parsley, and finely cut chives and basil
	salt and freshly ground pepper

○ Skin and trim the lamb. Cut into four pieces.

○ Boil up the veal and lamb stocks together, and allow to reduce by one-quarter.

○ Quickly blanch the onions, leek, cabbage and sprouts in boiling salted water. Remove and allow to drain.

○ Add the pieces of lamb to the reduced stock and allow to simmer for 2–3 minutes.

○ Add the blanched vegetables to the stock and simmer for 2–3 minutes.

○ Add the freshly chopped parsley, cut chives and basil, and season with salt and pepper.

○ Remove the vegetables and arrange in a suitable dish.

○ Just before serving, cut the meat into pieces approximately 1cm (less than $\frac{1}{2}$ in) thick and arrange on the vegetables. Serve immediately.

SAUTEED MIGNONS OF VEAL
WITH FRESH MARKET VEGETABLES

Mignons de veau aux légumes du marché

Any vegetables can be used in this recipe, according to the season. After blanching, cool the vegetables quickly in cold vegetable stock over ice.

4 PEOPLE

8	veal mignons, about 65g (2½ oz) each, well trimmed of all fat
50g (2 oz)	small mangetout, blanched for 10 seconds
100g (4 oz)	carrots, cut in strips and blanched for 20 seconds
100g (4 oz)	salsify, cut in strips and blanched for 20 seconds
50g (2 oz)	green beans, cut in half and blanched for 10 seconds
200g (7 oz)	fromage blanc (see page 33)
150g (5 oz)	low-fat natural yoghurt
25g (1 oz)	chives, finely cut
	salt and freshly ground pepper

○ Season the veal mignons with salt and pepper.

○ Sauté in a hot non-stick pan on each side for about 2–3 minutes, until still pink. Remove from pan and keep warm.

○ Dry the vegetables on kitchen paper, then sauté them in the same pan for about 1 minute. Season with salt and pepper.

○ Whisk together the fromage blanc and yoghurt and heat gently, whisking continually until light and frothy. (A hand sauce-maker/mixer is perfect for this.)

○ Season to taste with chives, salt and pepper.

○ Pour sauce on to four individual serving plates, garnish with the vegetables, then place the meat on top.

Sautéed Mignons of Veal with Fresh Market Vegetables (see page 128)

Fillet of Beef with Rosemary and Mustard (see page 123)

COLD LOIN OF VEAL
WITH BASIL SAUCE

Longe de veau froide au basilic

Turkey or breast of chicken can be prepared in this way as well. The sauce
may be enhanced with small cubes of red pepper.

4 PEOPLE

500g (1 lb, 2 oz)	loin of veal in one piece, bone and excess fat removed
100g (4 oz)	carrots, peeled and diced
50g (2 oz)	celeriac, peeled and diced
1	clove of garlic, unpeeled
1	small bay leaf
$\frac{1}{2}$	clove
425ml ($\frac{3}{4}$ pt)	white veal stock (see page 24)
100g (4 oz)	tomatoes, skinned, seeded and diced
10ml (2 tsp)	freshly cut basil
15ml (1 tbsp)	freshly chopped parsley
150g (5 oz)	fromage blanc (see page 33)
	juice of $\frac{1}{2}$ lemon
100g (4 oz)	onions, peeled and cut in half
	salt and freshly ground pepper

○ Simmer the meat in a non-stick pan together with the carrots, celeriac, garlic clove, bay leaf, clove, onions and veal stock, seasoned with salt and pepper, for 30 minutes until just cooked.

○ Allow to cool in the stock.

○ Reduce 200ml (7 fl. oz) of the stock to half its volume and put to one side for the sauce.

○ Put half of the basil, with all the parsley, the reduced stock plus the vegetables and skinned soft garlic clove into the mixer and purée.

○ Add the fromage blanc and mix in well, then season with salt, pepper and lemon juice.

○ Very thinly slice the veal, and arrange on a serving dish or directly on to individual plates, in a ring.

○ Cover with the well-seasoned sauce and sprinkle with the remaining basil.

○ Arrange tomato dice attractively in the middle of the dish or plate.

STEAMED CALF'S SWEETBREADS
Ris de veau à la vapeur

4 PEOPLE

550g (1¼ lb)	fresh calf's sweetbreads
300ml (½ pt)	white veal stock, well seasoned (see page 24)
40g (1½ oz)	onion, diced
25g (1 oz)	carrot, diced
25g (1 oz)	leek, diced
25g (1 oz)	celery, diced
1	small bay leaf
	a few sprigs of parsley
14	basil leaves
65g (2½ oz)	lean cooked ham, cut into thick strips
	salt and freshly ground white pepper

○ Soak the sweetbreads for several hours in water, changing frequently.

○ Blanch the sweetbreads in boiling salted water for 2–3 minutes. Refresh in cold water, then remove the skin with a small sharp knife.

○ Put the veal stock in a saucepan with the vegetables, bay leaf, sprigs of parsley and six of the basil leaves.

○ Place a steamer on top and steam the sweetbreads and ham for 5 minutes.

○ Remove the sweetbreads and ham and keep warm.

○ Strain the stock and boil rapidly to reduce to one-third of its original volume. Season to taste.

○ Spoon the reduced stock on to a plate and arrange slices of sweetbread on top. Garnish with strips of ham and the remaining basil leaves.

SAUTEED CALF'S LIVER WITH GARLIC

Foie de veau sauté à l'ail

Any other liver could be used in this recipe, but calf's is by far the most tender. The Vitamin C of the barely cooked vegetables helps the assimilation of the iron in the liver.

4 PEOPLE

15ml (1 tbsp)	cornflour
15ml (1 tbsp)	lemon juice
1	egg white
15ml (1 tbsp)	soya sauce
300g (10 oz)	calf's liver, cut in strips
250g (9 oz)	mangetout
6	shallots or button onions
15ml (1 tbsp)	fresh ginger root, peeled and chopped
150ml (¼ pt)	brown veal stock (see page 26)
1	small clove of garlic, crushed
	freshly ground pepper

○ Mix together 2 teaspoons of the cornflour, the lemon juice, lightly beaten egg white and 1 teaspoon of the soya sauce.

○ Mix the liver strips with the marinade, and leave for 20 minutes.

○ Clean and top and tail the mangetout, and peel the shallots or button onions.

○ Cut the shallots in half lengthwise, and sauté gently in a non-stick pan, turning constantly, for 5 minutes over a gentle heat.

○ Add the mangetout and ginger and, stirring all the time, sauté until half cooked. The vegetables should remain crisp and not lose their colour; place to one side.

○ Sauté the liver with the marinade in a non-stick pan for 2–3 minutes, turning constantly, then remove from the pan.

○ Mix the remaining cornflour with the remaining soya sauce and stock. Add to the pan and boil up, stirring all the time, until the sauce is thickened.

○ Mix in the vegetables, add the liver, warm quickly, and season with crushed garlic and a little pepper.

BOILED VEAL TONGUE WITH CHIVE SAUCE

Langue de veau bouillie à la ciboulette

4 PEOPLE

1	veal tongue, about 675g (1½ lb)
3 litres (5¼ pt)	water
1	medium onion, peeled and sliced
½	bay leaf
1	small leek, trimmed and sliced
1	medium carrot, peeled and sliced
	salt and freshly ground pepper

Sauce

20g (¾ oz)	fresh chives, finely cut
100ml (4 fl. oz)	tongue stock, strained (see below)
225g (8 oz)	fromage blanc (see page 33) juice of ½ lemon Cayenne pepper salt and freshly ground pepper
8	lengths of chive, about 5cm (2 in), for garnish

○ Wash the tongue well. Place all the other ingredients for the stock – water, onion, bay leaf, leek and carrot – in a saucepan. Season with salt and pepper and bring to the boil.

○ Add the tongue and simmer gently for 1½ hours until tender, occasionally removing the fat from the top.

○ Remove the tongue from the stock, allow to cool a little, then peel off the skin with a sharp knife.

○ Remove the fat and any gristly parts from the root end of the tongue.

○ Return the tongue to the strained stock to keep warm.

○ For the sauce, finely liquidize half the cut chives in the measured stock.

○ Mix in the fromage blanc and remaining cut chives. Season to taste with lemon juice, Cayenne, salt and pepper. Warm very gently.

○ Remove the tongue from the stock and cut into thin diagonal slices. Arrange on a suitable plate, and serve with the sauce, garnished with pieces of chive.

MEDALLIONS OF PORK STUDDED WITH PRUNES

Médaillons de porc piqués aux pruneaux

4 PEOPLE

8	pork medallions (from the tenderloin), about 50g (2 oz) each, well trimmed of fat
8	prunes, soaked in hot China tea, and stones removed
150ml (¼ pt)	brown veal stock (see page 26)
50g (2 oz)	*each* of carrots and turnips, cut into julienne strips
	salt and freshly ground pepper
15ml (1 tbsp)	chopped parsley to garnish

○ Make two small holes in each piece of pork with a sharp knife.

○ Cut four of the prunes into four, and press two pieces into each medallion of pork. Season with salt and pepper.

○ Sauté the medallions slowly in a non-stick frying pan for 4–5 minutes, turning once. Remove from the pan and keep warm.

○ Add the veal stock to the pan and boil down until reduced to a syrupy glaze. Strain through a sieve, then check the seasoning.

○ Meanwhile, blanch the carrots, turnips and remaining prunes in boiling water for 30 seconds. Drain and season to taste.

○ Arrange the pork medallions, carrot, turnip and prunes on a plate.

○ Spoon sauce around the meat and sprinkle with chopped parsley. Serve immediately.

FILLET OF PORK
WITH CHINESE LEAVES
Filet de porc à la pékinoise

Ginger and coriander, both very aromatic and believed to aid digestion, are
good accompaniments for this stir-fried dish.

4 PEOPLE

450g (1 lb)	pork fillet, well trimmed of fat
1	small onion, chopped
1	clove of garlic, crushed
$\frac{1}{2}$	small cauliflower, cut into florets
2	large carrots, cut in thin strips
$\frac{1}{2}$	bunch of spring onions, cut into 2.5cm (1 in) lengths
$\frac{1}{2}$	head of Chinese leaves, cut into 2.5cm (1 in) strips
5ml (1 tsp)	grated fresh ginger root
60ml (4 tbsp)	white chicken stock (see page 23)
15ml (1 tbsp)	soya sauce
	freshly ground pepper
	fresh coriander leaves to garnish

○ Cut the pork fillet into thin strips. Season with pepper, and sauté in a non-stick pan for 2 minutes on each side, to seal and brown the strips. Remove from the pan.

○ Sauté the onion, garlic, cauliflower and carrot for 3 minutes.

○ Add the spring onions, Chinese leaves, ginger and chicken stock to the pan. Cover and simmer gently for 2–3 minutes.

○ Add the pork, and season to taste with soya sauce and freshly ground pepper.

○ Serve immediately, garnished with the coriander leaves.

POULTRY

Poultry is the domestic or fattened birds such as chicken, goose, duck, turkey, etc. All others are classified as game birds. Poultry meat contains protein, vitamins and minerals (iron and phosphorus), and the meat of young poultry is well known for being easy to digest. A distinction is made between white poultry meat such as chicken and turkey, and dark poultry meat such as duck and goose. The difference in colour does not affect the quality or nutrients.

Try to obtain free-range chickens – not from a battery – and the flavourful maize- or corn-fed chickens that are widely available now. Baby chickens, or poussins, are the smallest variety, the weight being between 300–450g (10–16 oz); they are good for grilling. Poulardes are specially bred hens weighing up to 3kg (6½ lb), and are the best for jointing, and for the breasts which feature so strongly in the following Cuisine Naturelle recipes.

The majority of the recipes are for chicken, the most popular bird because of its mild, pleasant flavour, and its versatility. (Poultry, in fact, is now eaten much more regularly than meat.) It is also the least fatty – and in all the recipes the skin, which does contain fat, is removed. Duck has a fattier meat, but again, with skin removed and served with an acidic accompaniment, it is delicious and easy to digest.

In place of some of the salt in the following recipes, why not use a pinch of the herb mixture for poultry on page 40 – this will cut down the need for salt seasoning.

CHICKEN SAUTE WITH FRESH GINGER

Sauté de poulet Mikado

4 PEOPLE

500g (1 lb, 2 oz)	chicken meat, skinned, boned and cut into cubes (both white and brown meat)
50g (2 oz)	red pepper, seeded and sliced
50g (2 oz)	green pepper, seeded and sliced
50g (2 oz)	carrots, thinly sliced
100g (4 oz)	leeks, thinly sliced
200g (7 oz)	beansprouts
20g ($\frac{3}{4}$ oz)	fresh ginger root, peeled and thinly sliced
30ml (2 tbsp)	soya sauce
20ml (4 tsp)	wine vinegar
10ml (2 tsp)	cornflour
200ml (7 fl. oz)	white chicken stock (see page 23) freshly ground pepper

○ Season the chicken with pepper and sauté in a non-stick frying pan for about 3 minutes, stirring frequently, until coloured on all sides.

○ Remove from the pan and keep warm.

○ Sauté the peppers and carrots for 2 minutes in a non-stick pan.

○ Add the leeks and beansprouts and sauté for 30–45 seconds longer.

○ Stir in the ginger, soya sauce and vinegar.

○ Dissolve the cornflour in the chicken stock and add to the pan. Add the chicken and stir continuously until it comes to the boil.

○ Season to taste with pepper and serve at once.

BABY CHICKEN
WITH GRILLED VEGETABLES

Poussin aux légumes grillés

If you wish, the chicken and vegetables may be marked with a red-hot skewer before grilling to give an attractive finish. This is a version of 'quadrillage'.

4 PEOPLE

4	baby chickens, about 350g (12 oz) each
225g (8 oz)	broccoli, trimmed and cut into small florets
100g (4 oz)	tiny new carrots, peeled, with some of the green top left on
225g (8 oz)	new potatoes, peeled and sliced
100g (4 oz)	tender leeks, cut into 5cm (2 in) lengths
100g (4 oz)	courgettes, unpeeled and sliced
	salt and freshly ground pepper

○ Cut the chickens down the back, press them flat and remove the backbones and skin. Season with salt and pepper.

○ Blanch the broccoli and carrots in boiling water for 1 minute.

○ Grill the chicken for 10–12 minutes under medium heat.

○ Grill all the vegetables under low heat for 5–8 minutes until tender.

○ Arrange the chickens on individual serving plates and garnish with the vegetables.

POACHED CHICKEN BREAST
WITH RAW SEASONAL VEGETABLES

Blanc de volaille poché aux crudités de saison

A yoghurt dressing can be used for the chicken instead of the suggested sauce.

4 PEOPLE

100g (4 oz)	carrots, peeled
100g (4 oz)	courgettes, trimmed
100g (4 oz)	raw beetroot, peeled
100g (4 oz)	yellow pepper, trimmed
100g (4 oz)	celery, trimmed
100g (4 oz)	radishes, trimmed
4	chicken breasts, about 150g (5 oz) each, skinned and well trimmed
425ml ($\frac{3}{4}$ pt)	white chicken stock (see page 23)
60ml (4 tbsp)	chives, cut in 1.25cm ($\frac{1}{2}$ in) lengths
	salt and freshly ground pepper

Sauce
100ml (4 fl. oz)	reduced white chicken stock (see below)
30ml (2 tbsp)	tarragon vinegar
10ml (2 tsp)	French mustard

○ Cut all the vegetables into very fine julienne strips (or coarsely grate them). Keep each vegetable separate.

○ Season the chicken breasts with salt and pepper, then poach them in the chicken stock for 4–5 minutes.

○ Remove the breasts from the stock and cool. Reduce the stock to 100ml (4 fl. oz), then whisk in the vinegar and mustard to make the sauce.

○ Moisten each pile of vegetables with a little of the sauce, reserving some for the chicken. Season to taste.

○ Arrange small mounds of each vegetable around the edge of each plate.

○ Place the chicken in the centre, spoon over a little of the remaining sauce, and sprinkle with cut chives. Serve immediately.

SAUTE OF CHICKEN
WITH MIXED PEPPERS AND HERBS

Sauté de poulet au mélange de piments

To ensure that this dish has a good colour, it is important not to over-cook the peppers.

4 PEOPLE

1	chicken, about 1.5kg (3½ lb)
50g (2 oz)	onions, sliced
1	clove of garlic, finely chopped
100g (4 oz)	fresh mushrooms
100g (4 oz)	*each* of red, green and yellow peppers, seeded and cut into quarters
400g (14 oz)	tomatoes, seeded and diced
550ml (1 pt)	brown poultry stock (see page 25)
	a few sprigs of fresh thyme, marjoram and rosemary, chopped
4	basil leaves, finely cut
	salt and freshly ground pepper
	a few sprigs of parsley, chopped, for garnish

○ The chicken should be drawn, wiped clean and divided into eight pieces. Remove the skin; season chicken pieces lightly.

○ Sauté the chicken in a non-stick pan for about 5 minutes. Remove from the pan.

○ Sauté the onions, garlic, mushrooms and peppers for 1–2 minutes, stirring constantly. Transfer to a larger oven-proof pan or dish.

○ Add the tomatoes, chicken pieces and poultry stock, and bring to the boil.

○ Add the thyme, marjoram, rosemary and basil, cover and cook in a medium oven at 190°C/375°F/Gas 5 for 10 minutes.

○ Remove the chicken and vegetables, keep warm, and reduce the sauce by rapid boiling. Adjust seasoning.

○ Arrange chicken and vegetables on a suitable dish or dishes. Spoon the sauce over, sprinkle with parsley and serve.

BREAST OF CHICKEN WITH SPINACH

Friand de volaille en papillote

4 PEOPLE

4	breasts of chicken, skinned and boned
300g (11 oz)	spinach leaves, thick stems removed
50g (2 oz)	carrots
50g (2 oz)	leeks ⎫ cut into fine julienne strips
50g (2 oz)	celeriac ⎭
100ml (4 fl. oz)	brown chicken stock (see page 25)
10ml (2 tsp)	sherry vinegar
	salt and freshly ground pepper

○ Remove the fillets from the underside of the chicken breasts.

○ Put the chicken breasts and fillets between plastic film and flatten them with a rolling pin.

○ Blanch the spinach in boiling salted water then drain and immediately dip in iced water. Drain well then squeeze out excess moisture with a kitchen towel.

○ Sauté the vegetable julienne in a non-stick pan over gentle heat for about 5 minutes, stirring all the time.

○ Cut four large squares of greaseproof paper. Place a chicken breast on each, top with the spinach, then the sautéed vegetables, and then add the fillet of chicken.

○ Season well. Sprinkle over the stock and vinegar.

○ Seal the edges of the paper carefully, then bake in the oven at 200°C/400°F/Gas 5 for 6 minutes.

○ Remove from the oven and serve at once. Open at the table for the full aroma to be appreciated.

CHICKEN FRICASSEE
WITH VINEGAR AND TOMATO

Fricassée de volaille au vinaigre et tomate

4 PEOPLE

1	chicken, about 2.2kg (4¾ lb), dressed and wiped
3	cloves of garlic, skinned and crushed
2.5ml (½ tsp)	white peppercorns, crushed
1	large tomato, skinned, seeded and diced
100ml (4 fl. oz)	red wine vinegar
200ml (7 fl. oz)	brown chicken stock (see page 25)
	salt and freshly ground pepper

○ Divide the chicken into eight and carefully remove the skin. Cut off the outside part of the wings and remove any fat. Season with salt and pepper.

○ In a non-stick frying pan sauté the chicken for about 4 minutes on each side.

○ Add the garlic, crushed peppercorns and tomato, and sauté for 1 minute further.

○ Add the vinegar and bubble for 1–2 minutes to evaporate.

○ Add the chicken stock, cover and simmer for about 2–3 minutes until the chicken is tender.

○ Remove the chicken from the pan and keep warm.

○ Bring the sauce to the boil and simmer gently to a thin sauce consistency. Season to taste.

○ Arrange the chicken on plates and pour a little sauce over each. Serve immediately.

CHICKEN HOT POT

Pot-au-feu de volaille

4 PEOPLE

1	chicken, about 2.2kg (4¾ lb)
2 litres (3½ pt)	white chicken stock (see page 23)
3	onions, peeled, each studded with 2 cloves
1	bay leaf
2	cloves of garlic, peeled
	a few white peppercorns
	a bunch of herbs (such as thyme, rosemary, parsley stalks)
4	small carrots, peeled
4	pieces of celery, about 5cm (2 in) in length
4	pieces of leek, about 5cm (2 in) in length
4	small onions, skinned
1	small celeriac, peeled and cut into quarters
	salt and freshly ground pepper
	sprigs of parsley to garnish

○ Bring a large saucepan of water to the boil. Add the chicken and bring back to the boil. Drain and allow to cool slightly.

○ In a large pan, boil up the chicken stock, onions, bay leaf, garlic, peppercorns and herbs. Simmer for 20 minutes.

○ Add the chicken and poach for 20 minutes.

○ Remove the chicken from the pan. Strain the stock, remove the fat with strips of paper towel, and return to the cleaned-out pan. Remove the skin from the chicken.

○ Return the chicken to the pan. Add the vegetables. Bring to the boil and simmer for 10 minutes. Strain and keep the chicken and vegetables warm.

○ Boil the chicken stock rapidly to reduce by half. Adjust seasoning to taste.

○ Cut the chicken into eight and arrange in soup plates with the vegetables. Pour over some stock and garnish with parsley sprigs. Serve at once.

CHICKEN SUPREME
WITH WATERCRESS SAUCE

Suprême de volaille belle de nuit

The vegetables for this dish, and the herb garnish, can be changed according to the season.

4 PEOPLE

4	chicken breasts, about 150g (5 oz) each, skinned, wing bone cleaned, but all other bones removed
150g (5 oz)	carrots, cut into fine julienne strips
150g (5 oz)	celery, cut into fine julienne strips
150g (5 oz)	fine green beans, cut in half lengthways
4	stalks of tarragon
	salt and freshly ground pepper
4	sprigs of fresh tarragon to garnish

Sauce

400ml (14 fl. oz)	white chicken stock (see page 23)
100g (4 oz)	watercress leaves
50g (2 oz)	fromage blanc (see page 33)
75ml (5 tbsp)	chicken or meat glaze (see page 29)
	salt and freshly ground pepper

○ Season the chicken breasts with salt and pepper. Place in a steamer.

○ Put the vegetables and tarragon stalks on top and steam for 4–5 minutes. Remove tarragon stalks and keep chicken warm.

○ For the sauce, place 100ml (4 fl. oz) of the chicken stock in a pan with the watercress leaves. Bring to the boil.

○ Allow to cool, then purée in a liquidizer and pass through a sieve.

○ Boil the remaining chicken stock to reduce by half.

○ Whisk the fromage blanc and watercress purée into the reduced stock. Adjust seasoning to taste.

○ Pour the sauce on to four individual plates.

○ Warm the chicken or meat glaze and place in a small greaseproof paper piping bag. Snip off the end and pipe three concentric circles of glaze on the sauce.

○ Using a skewer, draw it across the sauce from the outside edge to the centre at regular intervals to give an attractive effect.

○ Place the chicken breasts carefully in the centre of each plate and garnish with tarragon.

Chicken Suprême with Watercress Sauce (see page 144)

Poached Chicken Breast with Raw Seasonal Vegetables (see page 139)

CHICKEN BREASTS WITH SPRING ONIONS

Délice de volaille grillé aux ciboules

4 PEOPLE

100g (4 oz)	spring onions, trimmed and chopped
25g (1 oz)	fresh ginger root, peeled and chopped
10ml (2 tsp)	chopped garlic
	pared rind and juice of 1 lemon
4	chicken breasts, skinned and boned
400ml (14 fl. oz)	white chicken stock (see page 23)
	salt and freshly ground pepper

○ Mix together three-quarters of the spring onions, and the ginger, garlic, lemon rind, salt and pepper. Add the chicken breasts, cover and marinate in the refrigerator for at least 12 hours, or up to 24 hours.

○ Pick out the lemon rind and blanch it in boiling water for 3 minutes. Cut into fine julienne strips.

○ Scrape the flavouring ingredients from the chicken and place them in a saucepan with the stock. Bring to the boil, cover and simmer for 10 minutes. Strain, pressing with a spoon to extract all the liquid. Return the stock to a small pan and boil for 10–15 minutes until reduced to about 100ml (14 fl. oz).

○ Remove from the heat. Stir in the remaining spring onions, the lemon rind julienne, and lemon juice to taste. Season to taste with salt and pepper.

○ Grill the chicken breasts for about 4–5 minutes each side until cooked through but still moist.

○ Warm the sauce gently, adding a little extra stock if necessary. Cut the chicken into 1.5cm ($\frac{1}{2}$ in) slices, crosswise on the diagonal. Fan out on a serving plate and spoon the sauce around the meat.

MARINATED LEMON CHICKEN

Poularde pochée au citron naturelle

This is a very simple recipe which can be served cold or hot. If cold, serve with a salad – Nettle Salad or Salade du Jardin would be ideal – and if hot, with a Rice Pilaff.

4 PEOPLE

1	poularde, about 2.2kg (4¾ lb), dressed and wiped clean

Marinade

2 litres (3½ pt)	white chicken stock (see page 23)
	juice and grated peel of 1 lemon
	salt and freshly ground pepper

Sauce

1	piece of lemon peel, finely chopped
1	clove
2	fresh mint leaves
40g (1½ oz)	*each* of carrots, leeks and celery, cut into small dice
4	mint sprigs to garnish

○ Boil up the ingredients for the marinade in a pan, put in the prepared chicken, and simmer for 30 minutes.

○ Allow to cool and marinate for about 3 hours.

○ Remove the chicken from the stock, and put to one side. Skim the stock and pass through a sieve.

○ Reduce the stock to two-thirds of its original volume.

○ Add the lemon peel, clove and mint leaves to the stock and reduce to about 300ml (½ pt) for the sauce.

○ Strain, add the vegetables, and bring back to the boil. Taste and add seasoning if necessary.

○ Divide the chicken into eight, remove skin, and warm through in the sauce.

○ Place each portion of chicken on a warmed plate and serve with the well-seasoned sauce. Garnish with mint sprigs.

GRILLED BREAST OF DUCK WITH APPLES

Suprême de canard grillé aux pommes fruits

The recipe uses two whole ducks, but it may be more convenient to buy
breasts. The apple served with the duck helps to counteract any residual
richness, and aids digestion.

4 PEOPLE

2	ducks, about 2.3kg (5 lb) each
200ml (7 fl. oz)	brown duck stock (see below and page 25)
15ml (1 tbsp)	green peppercorns, carefully selected and blanched
90ml (6 tbsp)	natural apple juice
1	eating apple, peeled, cored and cut into eight crescents
	salt and freshly ground pepper

○ Pluck the ducks clean and draw them. Cut off the head and neck, and remove the legs carefully (keep for use in another dish). Remove breasts.

○ Cut out the collarbone and backbone and chop into small pieces. Use these, with the neck, to make the brown duck stock.

○ Boil the measured stock until reduced by half. Add the blanched peppercorns.

○ Trim the breasts, and remove skin and bones. Season and cook under a medium grill for 6–7 minutes, turning once.

○ Warm the apple juice in a saucepan. Add the apples and simmer gently for 2–3 minutes until just tender.

○ Arrange the duck breasts on a plate and garnish with the apple pieces and peppercorns, drained from the stock.

○ Spoon a little warmed reduced duck stock around each piece of meat, and serve immediately.

GAME AND GAME BIRDS

Game is the term used for the meat of wild animals and birds. Deer and hare are the most common ground game, and their meat is nutritionally as good as other animals, tender and easily digestible.

The meat of feathered game - partridge, pheasant, wild duck and guinea fowl - is less rich in fat than that of domestic birds (the reason why it can so easily become dry if sautéed or grilled for too long). The flesh has a deeper and stronger taste than poultry (thus good stocks can be made from the carcasses). Young birds have soft breast bones, beaks that are not too hard, and down under the feathers.

Because close seasons exist by law, fresh game is only available for a limited time, and is at its best in the autumn. Britain has some of the best game in Europe, and as the season is so short, we all ought to make the most of the gastronomic delights game offers. Find a good supplier, to ensure the best quality.

Contrary to general opinion, game should not be hung for too long, or until over-ripe, as it loses some of its essential flavour.

Use a little game herb mixture (see page 40) in the following recipes to cut down on the salt content.

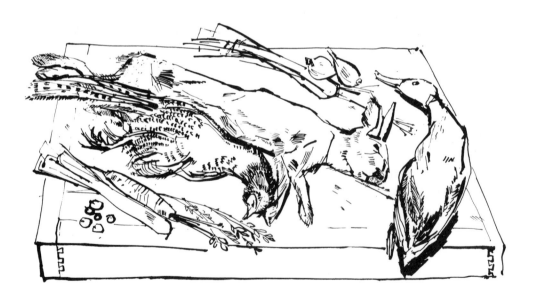

BREAST OF PHEASANT WITH ALMONDS

Délice de faisan aux amandes

The best time for eating pheasant, the most popular game bird, is from October until the end of December. Prepare while fresh or after hanging for a couple of days.

4 PEOPLE

2	young pheasants
100ml (4 fl. oz)	game stock (see page 28)
50g (2 oz)	flaked almonds, toasted in the oven
	salt and freshly ground pepper

Sauce

15g ($\frac{1}{2}$ oz)	shallot, peeled and finely diced
25g (1 oz)	celery, trimmed and finely diced
25g (1 oz)	carrot, peeled and finely diced
$\frac{1}{2}$	bay leaf
1	small sprig of thyme
750ml ($1\frac{1}{4}$ pt)	game stock (see page 28)

○ Remove the breasts from the pheasants, and reserve carcasses and legs for the sauce.

○ To make the sauce, chop the carcasses, legs and necks into small pieces, and place in a roasting tin.

○ Brown well in the oven at 150°C/300°F/Gas 2 for about 40 minutes.

○ Add the sauce vegetables and herbs, stir well and return to the oven for a further 10 minutes. Remove from the oven.

○ Add one-third of the stock and allow to simmer on top of the stove, uncovered, until of a syrupy consistency. Add another third of the stock and repeat the boiling down process.

○ Add the remainder of the stock and boil down to 150ml ($\frac{1}{4}$ pt). Strain and season to taste.

○ Trim the pheasant breasts, season with salt and pepper, and sauté in a non-stick frying pan for about 5–6 minutes, turning once. Remove from pan and keep warm.

○ Pour off any fat from the pan, and add the 100ml (4 fl. oz) game stock. Bring to the boil and reduce by half, then add to the sauce. Keep warm.

○ Cut the pheasant breasts carefully into thin slices.

○ Arrange on a suitable dish and sprinkle with flaked almonds. Serve the sauce separately.

WARM GUINEA FOWL
WITH CABBAGE SALAD

Pintade tiède à la salade de choux

4 PEOPLE

2	guinea fowl, about 900g (2 lb) each
225g (8 oz)	white cabbage, shredded
225g (8 oz)	Savoy cabbage, shredded
45ml (3 tbsp)	red wine vinegar
40g (1½ oz)	Parma ham, cut into julienne strips
	a selection of washed and dried salad leaves, such as lamb's lettuce, curly endive, chicory, radicchio, and julienne of carrot (blanched)
	salt and freshly ground pepper

○ Bone the guinea fowl and remove the skin. Reserve the breasts and slice the leg meat.

○ Sauté the sliced meat in a non-stick pan for about 2 minutes. Remove and keep warm.

○ Sauté the breasts in the non-stick pan for about 4–5 minutes, turning once, until golden. Remove from the pan and keep warm.

○ Add the cabbages to the pan and sauté for 2–3 minutes, stirring constantly. Add the vinegar.

○ Combine the Parma ham and sliced meat with the cabbages, and season to taste.

○ Place the salad leaves on four individual plates and arrange the cabbage salad on top.

○ Cut the guinea fowl breasts into thin slices and arrange in a fan on the top of each salad. Serve immediately.

BREAST OF GUINEA FOWL
WITH LEEK AND WILD MUSHROOMS

Suprême de pintade aux fruits des bois

Depending on seasonal availability, different varieties of mushrooms can
be used in this dish.

4 PEOPLE

4	breasts of guinea fowl, about 150g (5 oz) each, wing bones cleaned and trimmed
20g ($\frac{3}{4}$ oz)	shallots, finely chopped
200g (7 oz)	oyster mushrooms ⎱cleaned, washed and
150g (5 oz)	chanterelles ⎰cut in half
300g (11 oz)	leeks, cut in 5cm (2 in) lengths and blanched for 30 seconds salt and freshly ground pepper a few sprigs of chervil to garnish

○ Season the guinea fowl breasts with salt and pepper.

○ Sauté them in a non-stick frying pan for about 3 minutes, turning once. Remove from the pan and keep warm.

○ Add the finely chopped shallots to the pan and sauté, stirring constantly, until transparent. Remove from the pan and reserve.

○ Add the oyster mushrooms and chanterelles to the hot pan and sauté for about 1 minute.

○ Add the well-drained leeks and stir constantly for a further minute.

○ Return the shallots to the pan and season with salt and pepper.

○ Place the guinea fowl breasts on the vegetables in the pan, cover with foil, and heat gently for a further minute.

○ Arrange on four individual plates and garnish with sprigs of chervil.

PARTRIDGE WRAPPED IN LETTUCE LEAVES

Perdreau sauté au feuilles de laitue

Handle the breasts with care, and sauté until just pink for maximum tenderness.

4 PEOPLE

8	large Cos lettuce leaves
8	partridge breasts, skinned and well trimmed
150ml ($\frac{1}{4}$ pt)	game stock (see page 28)
1	small onion, skinned and finely chopped
50g (2 oz)	fresh mushrooms, sliced
	Cayenne pepper
	a squeeze of lemon juice
	salt and freshly ground pepper

○ Blanch the lettuce leaves in boiling water for 30 seconds. Dip in ice-cold water then drain well on kitchen paper or a teatowel.

○ Remove the thick, central stalk from the leaves.

○ In a non-stick frying pan, seal the seasoned partridge breasts quickly on both sides. Wrap each one in a lettuce leaf.

○ Place the lettuce packages in a gratin dish, and pour over the stock. Cover and place in a pre-heated oven at 200°C/400°F/Gas 6 for 4–5 minutes. Strain, retain the stock, and keep the packages warm.

○ For the sauce, sauté the onion in a non-stick pan for 1–2 minutes without browning. Add the mushrooms and continue to sauté for a further 1–2 minutes.

○ Add the stock strained from the partridge, and simmer for 1 minute. Season to taste with Cayenne, lemon juice, salt and pepper.

○ Spoon a little sauce on to each of four plates. Cut the lettuce packages in diagonal slices and fan out on the sauce. Serve immediately.

Breast of Guinea Fowl with Leek and Wild Mushrooms (see page 151)

Medallions of Hare with Grapes (see page 154)

WILD DUCK WITH ONION CONFIT

Canard sauvage aux oignons rouges

4 PEOPLE

4	breasts of wild young duck, skinned and trimmed
150g (5 oz)	red onions, finely sliced
45ml (3 tbsp)	red wine vinegar
300ml (½ pt)	wild duck stock (use carcass and legs, and see also page 28)
15-30ml (1–2 tbsp)	clear honey
	salt and freshly ground pepper

○ Lightly grill the seasoned wild duck breasts until pink, about 4–5 minutes. Keep warm.

○ Meanwhile sweat the onions in a non-stick pan until light brown, stirring constantly.

○ Add the red wine vinegar and reduce by half.

○ Add the duck stock and reduce by half.

○ Add honey to the sauce to taste, and season well with salt and pepper.

○ Cut the breasts of duck lengthways into 6mm (¼ in) slices.

○ Pour the sauce on to four warmed plates and lay the slices of duck on top. Serve immediately.

MEDALLIONS OF HARE WITH GRAPES

Médaillons de lièvre aux raisins

Prime quality hares are about 4–8 months, with a paler meat than older
animals.

4 PEOPLE

20	medallions of young hare (cut from the saddle), about 25g (1 oz) each, well trimmed and any sinews removed
40g (1½ oz)	shallots, finely chopped
6	juniper berries, roughly crushed
15g (½ oz)	thyme leaves
6	black peppercorns, roughly crushed
400ml (14 fl. oz)	game stock (see page 28)
20	large white grapes, skinned, and pips removed with a skewer
10ml (2 tsp)	lemon juice
150g (5 oz)	chanterelles, cleaned and washed
	salt and freshly ground pepper

○ Season the medallions of hare with salt and pepper.

○ Sauté them in a non-stick pan for about 2 minutes on each side until pink. Remove from the pan and keep warm.

○ Add the shallots to the pan and sauté, stirring constantly, until transparent.

○ Add the juniper berries, thyme leaves and peppercorns. Mix well and sauté for 1 minute.

○ Add the game stock and boil rapidly to reduce by half.

○ Strain the sauce and season to taste.

○ Place the grapes in a minimum of water flavoured with the lemon juice, and heat gently for 1 minute.

○ Sauté the prepared chanterelles in a non-stick pan, stirring all the time, for 1 minute. Season to taste.

○ Arrange five medallions of hare on each of four individual plates. Spoon the sauce over the meat.

○ Arrange the chanterelles in the centre of the meat and garnish with the well-drained grapes.

GRILLED MIGNONS OF VENISON WITH CRANBERRIES

Mignons de chevreuil grillés aux airelles

Venison is a very lean meat. It is relatively low in calories and high in iron and some vitamins. Animals under about 2 years have tender and easily digestible meat, while older animals are tougher.

4 PEOPLE

12	mignons of venison, about 40g (1½ oz) each, well trimmed
50ml (2 fl. oz)	orange juice
	juice of ½ lemon
10ml (2 tsp)	honey
200g (7 oz)	cranberries, washed
15g (½ oz)	shallots, finely chopped
300g (11 oz)	small chanterelles, cleaned, washed and dried
5ml (1 tsp)	finely chopped thyme
2.5ml (½ tsp)	finely cut sage
300ml (½ pt)	game stock (see page 28), reduced by half
	salt and freshly ground pepper

○ Season the mignons on both sides.

○ Grill them at a high temperature for 1 minute on each side, and keep warm.

○ Bring the orange and lemon juices and honey to the boil.

○ Add the cranberries and simmer for 30 seconds.

○ Sauté the shallots in a non-stick pan until transparent, stirring constantly.

○ Add the well-dried chanterelles and sauté for about 2 minutes. Season to taste.

○ Add the thyme and sage to the reduced stock, and arrange this sauce on four individual plates.

○ Place the mignons, three each, on the sauce, and put 5ml (1 tsp) of cranberries on each of the mignons.

○ Garnish with the chanterelles and serve immediately.

VEGETABLES

Vegetables should - and do - play a very large part in the preparation and presentation of a wide range of dishes. Many vegetables are colourful and of wonderful shapes, and add immeasurably to the finished look of a dish. Their flavours, too, are natural and subtle, complementing many other foods.

But the principal value of vegetables lies in their nutritional content. They are a major source of cellulose or fibre which is recognized as vital for health; and they also contain many vitamins and minerals not freely available from other foods.

To retain their benefits, however, vegetables need careful handling. Obviously the fresher the better; Vitamins A, C, B_1 and B_2 decrease daily after a vegetable is taken from the ground or plucked from the plant. They should never be stored for long. Cleaning, washing, and preparation are other danger areas. Vitamin C is water soluble, so may leach out if the vegetable is soaked; Vitamins B_1 and B_2 and some minerals (calcium, for example) may also be thus lost. Vegetables should also be cut or chopped just before use, as many lose their nutrients through contact with air as well as water - it is the Vitamin C oxidizing that turns potatoes (as well as fruits like apples) brown after being cut. This also affects flavour.

All previous efforts are wasted, however, if mistakes are made during cooking. Most vitamins and minerals will be lost if the vegetable is boiled for too long. (For this reason, it is always advisable to utilize vegetable water and its nutrients - in stocks, for instance.) Savoy cabbage boiled until it has lost its colour would lose 65 per cent of its Vitamin C content, and cauliflower 90 per cent (the latter is a good source of phosphorus, which would also be lost). If, however, the vegetables were steamed, approximately 80 per cent of their Vitamin C would be retained. Vegetables, to sum up, should be handled with the utmost care to protect their nutrients, colour, flavour and shape. Barely cook them so that they still remain crisp and delicious, unless using them for a purée.

Rice, millet and lentils are also used as vegetable accompaniments, and they are high in food value, containing protein and fibre. Many of the healthiest cuisines in the world have a basis in pulses and grains such as these. Brown rice is rice in its natural state after the husks have been removed; it has a stronger taste and is easier to digest than white rice, but takes longer to cook. Millet, another cereal plant, comes in many varieties and is a major world food crop. The best lentils are the brown and green varieties, and lentils are one of the three most popular pulses eaten in Europe.

Use a herb mixture (see page 40) in place of some seasoning to cut down on salt content.

STUFFED TOMATOES WITH SPINACH

Tomates farcies aux épinards

Serve these tomatoes on their own as a vegetable accompaniment, or as a
first course, arranged in soup plates with yellow pepper sauce.

4 PEOPLE

4	medium ripe tomatoes, stalks removed
20g (¾ oz)	shallots, finely chopped
200g (7 oz)	leaf spinach, stalks removed,
	blanched and roughly chopped
50g (2 oz)	cottage cheese
4	sprigs of chervil
	salt, nutmeg and freshly ground pepper

Yellow pepper sauce (optional, see above)

2	medium yellow peppers, washed and trimmed
15ml (1 tbsp)	finely chopped shallots
1	small clove of garlic, skinned and chopped
	a few sprigs of fresh thyme
400ml (14 fl. oz)	vegetable stock (see page 30)
	a pinch of sugar
	salt and freshly ground pepper

○ Cut open the stalk end of each tomato with a knife, take out the middle with a
teaspoon and season the tomatoes with salt.

○ Sauté the shallots in a non-stick pan, stirring carefully, until they are soft and
transparent but not coloured.

○ Add the well-drained spinach and sauté for about 2 minutes.

○ Add the cottage cheese and season with salt, nutmeg and pepper.

○ Carefully fill the tomatoes with the spinach mixture.

○ Place in an oven-proof non-stick pan, cover with foil and heat in a moderate oven
(180°C/350°F/Gas 4) for about 4–5 minutes.

○ If you wish to serve the tomatoes with the yellow pepper sauce, cut the peppers into
large pieces. Sweat the shallots and garlic in a non-stick pan over gentle heat without
browning. Add the yellow peppers, thyme and vegetable stock, and simmer,
uncovered, for about 20 minutes until pepper is tender. Liquidize and season to taste
with sugar, salt and pepper.

○ Serve as required (see above), garnished with a sprig of chervil.

LEAF SPINACH WITH CURD CHEESE

Epinards en feuilles Palace

4 PEOPLE

200g (7 oz)	young spinach, without stalks
15g ($\frac{1}{2}$ oz)	shallot, finely chopped
1	clove of garlic, unskinned
50g (2 oz)	curd cheese
	salt, freshly ground pepper
	and nutmeg

○ Wash the spinach leaves well, then dry.

○ Sweat the finely chopped shallot and the whole garlic clove carefully in a non-stick pan without colouring them.

○ Add the spinach leaves and sweat well for 3–4 minutes.

○ Add the curd cheese, and stir through.

○ Season with salt, freshly ground pepper and nutmeg.

○ Remove the clove of garlic before serving.

VEGETABLE GOULASH
WITH ROSEMARY AND MARJORAM

Goulasch de légumes aux herbes

Marrow or pumpkin, green or yellow peppers – whatever is colourful and
available – can be used in this flexible recipe.

4 PEOPLE

50g (2 oz)	onions, sliced
2	large tomatoes, skinned and chopped
150g (5 oz)	courgettes, sliced
150g (5 oz)	red pepper, cut and diced
1	clove of garlic, skinned and crushed
2.5ml ($\frac{1}{2}$ tsp)	tiny rosemary sprigs
2.5ml ($\frac{1}{2}$ tsp)	marjoram leaves
	salt and freshly ground pepper

○ Sauté the onions carefully in a non-stick pan, stirring constantly, until transparent but
not browned.

○ Add the tomatoes, courgettes and red pepper.

○ Stir in the garlic and herbs.

○ Cover and simmer for 3–4 minutes until just tender.

○ Season to taste with salt and pepper, and serve immediately.

COURGETTES WITH LETTUCE
AND SORREL SAUCE

Courgettes, sauce à la laitue et à l'oseille

4 PEOPLE

$\frac{1}{2}$	small onion, finely chopped
$\frac{1}{2}$	round lettuce, cut into strips
30ml (2 tbsp)	fresh sorrel, cut into strips
200ml (7 fl. oz)	white chicken stock (see page 23)
100g (4 oz)	cottage cheese, sieved
1	egg yolk
450g (1 lb)	courgettes, thinly sliced
	salt and freshly ground pepper

○ Sauté the onion, lettuce and sorrel, stirring gently for 2–3 minutes, in a non-stick pan.

○ Add the stock and simmer, covered, for 5–6 minutes. Blend in a liquidizer.

○ Return to the pan and stir in the cottage cheese mixed with the egg yolk; heat gently, stirring, until thickened. Do not let the sauce boil. Season to taste with salt and pepper.

○ Steam the courgettes for 2–3 minutes. Season with salt and pepper.

○ Pour the sauce on to a plate, and arrange the courgette slices on top.

SAUTEED PARSNIPS WITH SESAME SEEDS

Panais sautés aux sésames

The sweetness of the parsnips combines interestingly with the nutty
flavour of the sautéed sesame seeds – which are high in protein, and a good
source of B vitamins and minerals.

4 PEOPLE

15ml (1 tbsp)	sesame seeds
450g (1 lb)	parsnips, peeled, quartered lengthwise, and thinly sliced
4	spring onions, cut in 2.5cm (1 in) pieces
1	clove of garlic, peeled and chopped
100g (4 oz)	mangetout, trimmed and cut in half lengthwise
	salt and freshly ground pepper

○ Sauté the seeds carefully until golden brown in a non-stick pan.

○ Add the parsnips, spring onion pieces and garlic, and sauté for 5 minutes until just tender.

○ Add the mangetout and sauté for another 1 minute.

○ Season to taste with salt and pepper, and serve immediately.

CHICORY AND MUSHROOMS GLAZED WITH CHEESE

Endives Belges et champignons gratinés

4 PEOPLE

4	large heads of chicory
150g (5 oz)	small button mushrooms
100ml (4 fl. oz)	white chicken or vegetable stock (see pages 23 or 30)
10ml (2 tsp)	lemon juice
5ml (1 tsp)	honey
50g (2 oz)	Gouda cheese, grated
	salt and freshly ground pepper

○ Wash the chicory well, cut off 1cm ($\frac{1}{2}$ in) at the bottom and then break into separate leaves. Place in a saucepan.

○ Place the mushrooms in another pan.

○ Divide the stock and lemon juice between the two pans. Add the honey to the chicory.

○ Cook the chicory quickly for 1–2 minutes until just tender. Drain and arrange in a small gratin dish.

○ Bring the chicory stock to the boil and boil rapidly to reduce to 15ml (1 tbsp). Spoon over the chicory.

○ Sauté the mushrooms quickly until no liquid remains.

○ Spoon the mushrooms over the chicory and season to taste.

○ Sprinkle with grated cheese and bubble under a hot grill until golden.

GLAZED SHALLOTS
Echalotes glacées

Spring onions or silver onions may be prepared in the same way as the shallots.

4 PEOPLE

200g (7 oz)	small shallots
100ml (4 fl. oz)	apple juice
200ml (7 fl. oz)	water
	salt and freshly ground pepper

○ Carefully remove the root part of the shallots, then peel them, leaving them whole.

○ Heat a non-stick pan, add the shallots and sweat over a low heat.

○ Add the apple juice and allow to caramelize by tipping the pan; do not stir.

○ Add the water and seasoning to taste

○ Cover and simmer over low heat for 10–12 minutes.

○ Remove the shallots and reduce the liquid to about 30ml (2 tbsp).

○ Replace the shallots in the sauce and serve immediately.

CARROT AND SPINACH MOUSSE

Mousseline de carottes et épinards

These mousseline shapes look and taste wonderful, and go well with any
meat dish.

4 PEOPLE

For carrot layer
225g (8 oz) carrots, thinly sliced
60ml (4 tbsp) tofu
1 egg white

For spinach layer
225g (8 oz) spinach leaves,
washed and
thick stalks removed
1 egg white
100ml (6–7 tbsp) tofu
freshly grated nutmeg
salt and freshly ground pepper

○ Cook the carrots in a minimum of boiling salted water until tender, about
3–4 minutes. Drain.

○ Add the tofu to the drained carrots and make into a purée. Season to taste with salt
and pepper.

○ Whisk the carrot egg white to a soft peak and fold into the purée.

○ Cook the spinach over a gentle heat without extra water, until tender and dry.

○ Mix with the tofu and make into a purée. Season with nutmeg, salt and pepper.
Whisk spinach egg white to a soft peak and fold into the purée.

○ Divide the carrot purée between four individual ramekin dishes, and level the
surface. Top with the spinach purée and level the surface.

○ Cover with foil and cook in a bain-marie in the oven at 180°C/350°F/Gas 4 for
25–30 minutes until just firm to the touch. (A wooden cocktail stick will come out of
the mousse clean when it is cooked.)

○ Cool slightly then invert on to a serving dish.

ARTICHOKE MOUSSE

Purée d'artichauts

This mousse goes well with meat dishes, particularly lamb.

4 PEOPLE

3	large globe artichokes
45ml (3 tbsp)	curd cheese
1	egg
5ml (1 tsp)	finely cut chervil leaves
	squeeze of lemon juice
	salt and freshly ground pepper

Sauce

30ml (2 tbsp)	curd cheese
100g (4 oz)	low-fat natural yoghurt
10ml (2 tsp)	finely cut chervil leaves
	pinch of Cayenne pepper
	salt
	parsley sprigs to garnish

○ Break off the stalks of the artichokes so that the tough fibres come away from the bottoms.

○ Cook the artichokes in lightly salted water for 30–40 minutes (they are cooked when the leaves can be pulled away easily).

○ When cool, take off the leaves, remove and discard the hairy choke, and chop the artichoke bottoms. Using a spoon, scrape the flesh from the base of each leaf.

○ Purée all the artichoke flesh with the curd cheese and egg. Stir in the chervil and season to taste with lemon juice, salt and pepper.

○ Spoon the mixture into four individual non-stick moulds. Cover with foil and cook in a bain-marie in the oven at 160°C/325°F/Gas 3 for 20–25 minutes until just firm to the touch. Allow to cool slightly.

○ Mix together all the ingredients for the sauce, bring to the boil and season well.

○ Unmould the mousses on to the centre of each of four plates. Spoon a little sauce around each one and garnish with parsley sprigs.

SWEETCORN GALETTE

Galette de maïs

These small pancakes make a very good accompaniment to grilled meat
and poultry. Sweetcorn contains fibre and Vitamin C.

4 PEOPLE

300g (11 oz)	corn on the cob
150ml ($\frac{1}{4}$ pt)	skimmed milk
100g (4 oz)	fromage blanc (see page 33)
1	egg
1	egg yolk
65g ($2\frac{1}{2}$ oz)	flour
	salt, a little freshly ground nutmeg and pepper

○ Wash the corn on the cob well and blanch in the milk.

○ Remove the corn from the cob and chop the kernels roughly. Keep the milk for the batter.

○ Mix together the milk, fromage blanc, egg, egg yolk and flour, by hand or in the blender. Do it fairly slowly to avoid lumps.

○ Add the roughly chopped corn and flavour with salt, nutmeg and pepper.

○ Heat a non-stick frying pan, measure out small pancakes with a tablespoon and sauté until golden brown on both sides.

RICE PILAFF

Riz pilaf

Rice is the largest food crop in the world. Brown – or whole – rice still has
the bran coating which is removed from white rice, and thus retains all the
valuable proteins and minerals as well as fibre.

4 PEOPLE

20g ($\frac{3}{4}$ oz)	onion, finely chopped
200g (7 oz)	brown long-grain rice
300ml ($\frac{1}{2}$ pt)	vegetable stock (see page 30)
	salt and freshly ground pepper

○ Sauté the onion carefully in a non-stick pan until transparent, stirring constantly.

○ Transfer to a suitable flame- and oven-proof casserole. Add the rice, vegetable stock
and seasoning to taste.

○ Bring to the boil on top of the stove, then cover with a piece of greaseproof paper and
a lid, and place in the oven at 180°C/350°F/Gas 4. Leave for about 20–25 minutes,
stirring occasionally.

○ Remove from the casserole, and taste for seasoning. Fluff up with a fork and serve
immediately.

VEGETABLE RICE
WITH TOASTED HAZELNUTS

Riz et légumes aux noisettes

Hazelnuts, most commonly used in cakes and sweet dishes, here lend their
flavour and goodness to a savoury rice accompaniment. They are lower in
calories than most other nuts.

4 PEOPLE

175g (6 oz)	hazelnuts
1	medium onion, peeled and chopped
1	clove of garlic, crushed
225g (8 oz)	brown long-grain rice
425ml ($\frac{3}{4}$ pt)	water
2.5ml ($\frac{1}{2}$ tsp)	turmeric
1	large carrot, scraped and diced
225g (8 oz)	French beans, cut into 5cm (2 in) pieces
1	small red pepper, seeded and finely cut
4	tomatoes, peeled and quartered
	salt and freshly ground pepper

○ Toast the nuts in the oven at 180°C/350°F/Gas 4 for about 10 minutes.

○ Sauté the onion and garlic in a non-stick pan, stirring constantly, until they are soft and transparent but not coloured.

○ Add the rice, water, turmeric and a little salt and bring to the boil. Cover and simmer very gently for about 30 minutes until the rice is tender.

○ Meanwhile, cook the carrot, beans and pepper in boiling salted water until tender, 3–5 minutes. Drain.

○ Using a fork, carefully mix the cooked vegetables and tomatoes into the rice, together with half the toasted hazelnuts. Season to taste with salt and pepper.

○ Serve in a large shallow dish, sprinkled with the remaining hazelnuts.

BRAISED LENTILS

Lentilles braisées

4 PEOPLE

250g (9 oz)	fresh brown lentils
100g (4 oz)	onions ⎫
40g (1½ oz)	carrots ⎬ finely cut
40g (1½ oz)	leeks ⎭
100g (4 oz)	potatoes, cut into small dice
40g (1½ oz)	tomato concasse (see page 37)
550ml (1 pt)	brown veal stock (see page 26)
1	small clove of garlic, whole and pressed
10ml (2 tsp)	wine vinegar
	salt and freshly ground pepper

○ Wash the lentils thoroughly, picking out stems and any that float.

○ Sauté the vegetables and tomato concasse in a non-stick pan, stirring all the time, for about 3–4 minutes. Add the veal stock and garlic.

○ Add the well-drained lentils, and bring to the boil.

○ Season with salt and pepper. Skim and simmer until just tender, about 20 minutes.

○ Remove the garlic.

○ Purée a quarter of the cooked lentils in a liquidizer and stir the rest of the lentils into the purée.

○ Finally, add the vinegar and season with salt and pepper.

MILLET PILAFF

Pilaf de millet

Millet is very mild in flavour, but combined with the ingredients below, it
provides a tasty accompaniment for meat, especially beef.

4 PEOPLE

250g (9 oz)	millet
1 litre (1¾ pt)	vegetable stock (see page 30)
15ml (1 tbsp)	fresh yeast
15ml (1 tbsp)	soya sauce
100g (4 oz)	curd cheese
	salt and freshly ground pepper

○ Place the millet in a non-stick pan over medium heat and sauté until golden coloured,
stirring occasionally, about 5–8 minutes.

○ Add the stock and simmer gently for 30–40 minutes until all the stock is absorbed and
the millet is tender.

○ Add the fresh yeast, stir in the soya sauce and cheese, and serve at once. Adjust
seasoning to taste.

YOUNG NETTLE AND POTATO PUREE

Purée d'orties et pommes de terre

Wherever man settles in the northern hemisphere, nettles appear. They are 'culture followers' and indicate nitrogenous ground. They are also full of goodness – containing several vitamins, tannin, mineral salts and iron – but only the youngest nettle tops must be used. Spinach leaves can replace some of the nettles in this recipe if liked.

4 PEOPLE

about 225g (8 oz)	young nettle tops
1	small potato, peeled and diced
about 425ml (¾ pt)	vegetable stock (see page 30)
100g (4 oz)	fromage blanc (see page 33)
	freshly grated nutmeg
	salt and freshly ground pepper

○ Pick the nettle tops carefully, preferably with gloves. Wash them well in salted water, then drain.

○ Place the nettles, potato and stock in a saucepan. Cover and simmer for 20 minutes, adding more stock if necessary.

○ Pour off any excess liquid and purée the mixture in a liquidizer.

○ Season the purée well with nutmeg, salt and pepper, then stir in the fromage blanc.

POTATOES WITH GOAT'S CHEESE

Pommes de terre au fromage de chèvre

By the time the potatoes are soft, the liquid has been absorbed, making a
wonderful soft, tasty accompaniment to many grilled meat dishes. Goat's
cheese gives it a different and special flavour, but other cheeses may be
used to reduce fat and calorie content.

4 PEOPLE

400g (14 oz)	medium potatoes, peeled and washed
1	small clove of garlic, peeled and cut in half
200ml (7 fl. oz)	vegetable stock (see page 30)
80g (3¼ oz)	soft goat's cheese, crushed into small pieces
	salt and freshly ground pepper

○ Cut the potatoes into 3mm ($\frac{1}{8}$ in) thick slices, then place on a cloth to dry. Season with
salt and pepper.

○ Rub a suitable gratin dish with the cut clove of garlic.

○ Arrange the potato slices in the dish in layers.

○ Add the vegetable stock and bake in the pre-heated oven at 190°C/375°F/Gas 5 for
about 30 minutes.

○ About 5 minutes before the end of cooking time, sprinkle the cheese over the
potatoes, return to the oven, and bake for a few minutes longer until golden brown.

POTATOES SAUTEED WITH HAM

Pommes de terre sautées au jambon

Parma ham or a smoked ham can be used instead of cooked ham. All fat must be removed from ham, whatever kind, before use. Serve with any meat dish.

4 PEOPLE

400g (14 oz)	medium potatoes, washed, peeled and grated
50g (2 oz)	onions, sliced
50g (2 oz)	cooked ham, without fat, cut into fine julienne strips
	salt and freshly ground pepper

○ Dry the potatoes thoroughly on a cloth.

○ Sauté the onion in a non-stick pan until transparent, stirring constantly.

○ Add the ham and sauté for 2 minutes.

○ Add the well-dried potatoes and season with salt and pepper. Sauté until light brown in colour.

○ Form the contents of the pan into a cake shape, using a palette knife. Press quite heavily so that the potato strips stick together.

○ Sauté the ham and potato 'cake' on both sides until golden brown.

JACQUELINE POTATOES

Pommes de terre Jacqueline

These attractive potato shapes are an ideal accompaniment for any meat dish, especially Fillet of Beef with Rosemary and Mustard (see page 123).

4 PEOPLE

400g (14 oz)	medium potatoes, peeled and washed
50g (2 oz)	fromage blanc (see page 33)
	salt, freshly ground pepper
	and nutmeg

○ Cut the potatoes into 3mm (⅛ in) slices, using a knife or a mandoline, then pat dry with a cloth.

○ Place in a bowl, add the fromage blanc, and season with salt, pepper and nutmeg. Mix well.

○ Using any small mould (little aluminium containers work well), one or more per person, depending on size, fill them with overlapping circles of potato slices coated with fromage blanc.

○ Bake in the oven at 190°C/375°F/Gas 5 for about 12 minutes.

○ Ease the potatoes out of the mould with a palette or small knife, and serve immediately.

DESSERTS

Desserts, sweets or puddings are synonymous in many people's minds with some of the excluded ingredients of Cuisine Naturelle - butter, cream and sugar, and thus pastry, chocolate and many other basics of the art of dessert preparation. However, by omitting butter and cream completely, and using yoghurt or quark instead, and by cutting down on traditional quantities of sugar, relying more on the natural sugars in fruit, for instance, the following desserts represent a good variety of healthy and delicious finales to any meal. And as they *are* the finale, the last memory of a wonderful meal, they must also *look* spectacular.

The majority of the recipes use fresh fruit in some form or another, served raw to conserve its abundant Vitamin C, or prepared simply in another way. There are ice-creams (made with yoghurt), sorbets, terrines and mousses. Soft fruits are made - with brown bread - into a magnificent summer pudding, or piled into the very lightest filo pastry strudel or a thin lacework tuile basket. And to complete the selection there is a trio of healthful petits fours.

APPLE SORBET

Sorbet de pomme fruit

4 PEOPLE

400g (14 oz)	dessert apples
200ml (7 fl. oz)	thick apple juice
	juice of 1 lime

○ Peel the apples, cut into quarters and remove the core, then slice.

○ Bring the apple juice and lime juice to the boil, and cook the apples in the liquid until soft.

○ Purée the apples and liquid in a liquidizer, cool and freeze. Whisk the ice vigorously from time to time, or transfer to a sorbetière and freeze.

MELON SORBET

Sorbet de melon

4 PEOPLE

250ml (9 fl. oz)	water
50g (2 oz)	sugar
400g (14 oz)	ripe melon
	juice of 1 lime

○ Bring the water and sugar to the boil. Allow to cool.

○ Divide the melon into eight, remove the seeds and skin, cut the flesh into cubes, and purée with the lime juice in a liquidizer.

○ Mix the fruit purée with the cold sugar and water mixture.

○ Freeze immediately, whisking the ice vigorously from time to time, or transfer to a sorbetière and freeze.

SPICED SORBET

Sorbet d'épices

This sorbet may be served after fish or between a fish and main dish,
providing the meal has more than four courses.
To vary the recipe, boil up a split vanilla pod, or 2 cinnamon sticks instead
of the saffron, with the water and sugar, cook for 1 minute and allow to
cool. Remove the vanilla pod or cinnamon sticks and continue as below.

4 PEOPLE

400ml (14 fl. oz)	water
80g (3¼ oz)	sugar
	a large pinch of saffron strands
45ml (3 tbsp)	lime juice
1	egg white

○ Bring the water, 50g (2 oz) of the sugar, and the saffron to the boil and cook for
1 minute, stirring constantly. Allow to cool.

○ Strain the lime juice and mix with the sugar syrup.

○ Whisk the egg white until stiff, then whisk in the remaining sugar.

○ Carefully fold the whipped egg white into the completely cooled liquid, and then
freeze, whisking the ice vigorously from time to time, or transfer to a sorbetière and
freeze.

BLACK SPOOM

A spoom is a sorbet with added egg whites, and black spoom is a sorbet made
with black tea. The tea should be infused; do not boil, or the fine flavour is lost
and it becomes bitter.
Try your own mixtures of teas. You can use Earl Grey, Darjeeling, Lapsang
Souchong or green China tea. You could also try herb, fruit or flower teas, such
as hawthorn blossom, elderflower, woodruff blossom, rosehip, fresh mint or
fresh lemon mint.

4 PEOPLE

400ml (14 fl. oz)	sparkling mineral water
30ml (2 tbsp)	black tea (flowery orange Pekoe quality)
75g (3 oz)	sugar
1-2	egg whites

- ○ Bring the mineral water to the boil.
- ○ Put the tea leaves into a jug and pour on the boiling water.
- ○ Let the tea infuse for 2 minutes.
- ○ Stir, strain the tea and add the sugar. Continue to stir until the sugar dissolves. Cool.
- ○ Beat the egg whites until stiff.
- ○ Carefully fold the egg whites into the completely cold liquid and freeze. Whisk the ice vigorously from time to time, or transfer to a sorbetière and freeze.

COFFEE GRANITE

Mocca Granité

Granité, gremolata or granita is nearest to the original sorbet – hardly sweetened, and with fairly large ice crystals. The thickness of the sorbet, and size of the ice crystals, depends on the amount of sugar or sweetening used, and on how much it is stirred during freezing.

4 PEOPLE

30ml (2 tbsp)	coffee beans, darkly roasted
400ml (14 fl. oz)	water, brought to the boil
30ml (2 tbsp)	clear honey

- ○ Coarsely grind the coffee beans or crush them in a mortar.
- ○ Put the coffee into a pan and pour on the boiling water.
- ○ Cover and put the pan in a warm bain-marie for 15 minutes to allow the coffee to brew.
- ○ Strain the coffee and immediately add the honey. Stir until the honey dissolves.
- ○ Allow the coffee syrup to cool.
- ○ Pour the cooled coffee syrup into a container and place in the freezer for 2–3 hours.
- ○ Stir every 30 minutes with a spoon.
- ○ Serve scooped into individual glasses.

YOGHURT FRUIT ICE

Glace de yogourt et fruits

In this and the following yoghurt ices, the cream or milk is replaced by
yoghurt which is much lower in calories. Goat's milk yoghurt could also be
used, but it is higher in fat and calorie content.

4 PEOPLE

225g (8 oz)	berries (strawberries, raspberries or other fruits)
30ml (2 tbsp)	lemon juice
75g (3 oz)	low-fat natural yoghurt
75g (3 oz)	caster sugar
75g (3 oz)	quark (see page 34)

○ Liquidize the fruits with the lemon juice.

○ Whisk together the yoghurt and caster sugar and mix with the fruit purée.

○ Beat the quark until smooth and carefully fold into the mixture.

○ Freeze immediately, whisking the ice vigorously from time to time, or transfer to a
sorbetière and freeze.

GOAT'S MILK YOGHURT
RASPBERRY ICE

Glace de yogourt de chèvre et framboise

Similar goat's milk yoghurt ices could be made with redcurrants and red
bilberries – and they all could, naturally, be made with ordinary low-fat
natural yoghurt.

4 PEOPLE

200g (7 oz)	raspberries
20g (¾ oz)	caster sugar
300g (10 oz)	goat's milk yoghurt (see page 35)
2	egg yolks
25g (1 oz)	caster sugar
45ml (3 tbsp)	water

- ○ Push the raspberries through a sieve and mix with the caster sugar and yoghurt.

- ○ Beat the egg yolks until creamy.

- ○ Boil the sugar and water together until the bubbles settle and flatten (118 °C/245 °F).

- ○ Using an electric whisk turned on full, gradually pour the hot syrup into the egg yolks and keep beating until the mixture is cold and thick.

- ○ Stir the egg-yolk cream with the yoghurt mixture, put into a 500ml (18 fl. oz) mould and freeze for 2–3 hours, whisking the ice vigorously from time to time. Before dividing into portions allow to thaw in the refrigerator for 20 minutes.

OATMEAL ICE-CREAM
Glace d'avoine

4 PEOPLE

50g (2 oz)	medium oatmeal
50g (2 oz)	caster sugar
2	egg yolks
150ml ($\frac{1}{4}$ pt)	skimmed milk
300ml ($\frac{1}{2}$ pt)	low-fat natural yoghurt
100g (4 oz)	raspberries, to decorate

- ○ Place the oatmeal in a non-stick pan and sauté over a gentle heat until golden brown. Remove from the pan and leave to cool.

- ○ Whisk together the sugar and egg yolks.

- ○ Heat the milk to blood temperature and stir into the egg mixture.

- ○ Place in a double-boiler, or in a basin over simmering water, and cook until the mixture is thick enough to coat the back of a wooden spoon. Cool.

- ○ Stir in the oatmeal and yoghurt.

- ○ Freeze immediately, whisking the ice vigorously from time to time.

- ○ Serve ice-cream in scoops, decorated with raspberries.

SYMPHONY OF FRUIT MOUSSES

Symphonie de mousses aux fruits

8 PEOPLE

Raspberry mousse

200g (7 oz)	raspberries, puréed and strained
2	eggs, separated
25g (1 oz)	caster sugar
2	leaves of gelatine, soaked in cold water and squeezed dry
50g (2 oz)	quark (see page 34)

Mango mousse

1	large mango, about 350g (12 oz), peeled, puréed and strained
2	eggs, separated
25g (1 oz)	caster sugar
2	leaves of gelatine (prepared as above)
5ml (1 tsp)	lemon juice
50g (2 oz)	quark (see page 34)

Lime mousse

	pared rind and strained juice of 3 limes
2	eggs, separated
25g (1 oz)	caster sugar
2	leaves of gelatine (prepared as above)
50g (2 oz)	quark (see page 34)

Mango sauce

1	mango, about 500g (1 lb, 2 oz), peeled and puréed
	lemon juice to taste

Raspberry sauce

300g (11 oz)	raspberries
20ml (4 tsp)	icing sugar
	lemon juice to taste

Garnish

8	raspberries, nice and ripe
24	mint leaves

The three mousses are made in the same way:

○ Whisk the egg yolks with the sugar in a basin over hot water until pale and thick.

○ Dissolve the gelatine in 30ml (2 tbsp) water.

○ Stir the gelatine into the fruit purée and add lemon juice if specified.

○ Whisk in the egg mixture and cool.

○ Whisk in the quark and chill until just beginning to set.

○ Whisk the egg whites until stiff.

○ Fold into the fruit mixture and chill until set.

○ To make the mango sauce, mix together the mango purée and a little water, and simmer gently for 2–3 minutes. Cool and stir in a little lemon juice to taste. Strain.

○ To make the raspberry sauce, purée and strain the raspberries. Stir in the icing sugar and lemon juice to taste. Reduce half the raspberry sauce by one-third to get a darker colour.

○ To serve, shape a quenelle of each mousse on to each plate. Pour a little of the mango sauce between each quenelle of mousse. Top with the lighter raspberry sauce and then the darker raspberry sauce. Garnish with a fresh raspberry and three mint leaves.

MANGO AND GRAPE MOUSSE

Mousse des mangues et raisins

This is a simple recipe, but very effective because of the unusual combination of fruits. The mango must be very ripe for the fullest flavour.

4 PEOPLE

1	large, ripe mango, about 600g (1 lb, 5 oz), peeled and diced
300g (11 oz)	black grapes, washed, halved and pipped
150g (5 oz)	low-fat natural yoghurt
175g (6 oz)	quark (see page 34)
30ml (2 tbsp)	caster sugar
25g (1 oz)	flaked almonds, toasted

○ Reserve a little mango and a few grapes for the decoration.

○ Add the remainder to a mixture of the yoghurt, quark and sugar. Mix in well.

○ Chill for about 2 hours.

○ Stir in the almonds, then spoon into four individual glasses. Decorate with the reserved fruit and serve immediately.

DATE AND APPLE MOUSSE

Mousse de dattes et pommes fruits

Toast the pine kernels on a roasting tray in the oven to bring out their nutty
taste. This is a very simple but effective recipe.

4 PEOPLE

675g (1½ lb)	cooking apples, peeled, cored and sliced
22.5ml (1½ tbsp)	lemon juice
45-75ml (3-5 tbsp)	honey
175g (6 oz)	fresh dates
15ml (1 tbsp)	pine kernels, toasted
4	mint sprigs to decorate

○ Place the apple slices in a pan with the lemon juice and 30ml (2 tbsp) water. Cover and cook over a very gentle heat for 10-15 minutes until soft, stirring occasionally.

○ Sieve the apples to make a smooth purée, then stir in the honey to taste.

○ Skin and remove the stones from the dates. Cut into thin strips. Stir into the apple purée.

○ Chill the purée, if wished, or serve lukewarm in glasses, sprinkled with pine kernels and decorated with mint sprigs.

Sorbets (see pages 177-8)

Small Fruit Baskets with Raspberry and Peach Sauces (see pages 190-1)

Terrine of Oranges with Raspberry Sauce (see pages 186-7)

A Symphony of Fruit Mousses (see pages 182-3)

SUMMER FRUITS WITH VANILLA SAUCE

Délice des fruits d'été

This can be made with any fruit – red or black cherries, strawberries, loganberries, bilberries, etc., and instead of the vanilla sauce, you could serve quark. This looks pretty served in goblets.

10 PEOPLE

200g (7 oz)	raspberries
200g (7 oz)	blackberries
100g (4 oz)	gooseberries
100g (4 oz)	redcurrants
100g (4 oz)	blackcurrants
100g (4 oz)	sugar
50g (2 oz)	cornflour

Red berry juice

200g (7 oz)	raspberries
200g (7 oz)	redcurrants
550ml (1 pt)	water

Vanilla sauce

2	egg yolks
20g ($\frac{3}{4}$ oz)	sugar
250ml (9 fl. oz)	skimmed milk
1	vanilla pod, split

○ Only wash the berries if necessary. Rinse in a sieve a few at a time, allow to drain, and dry with kitchen paper.

○ Remove the stalks from the berries.

○ To make the red berry juice, boil up the raspberries, redcurrants and water, then simmer over a gentle heat for 5 minutes. Push the berries through a sieve.

○ Boil up the red berry juice and the 100g (4 oz) sugar until the sugar has dissolved.

○ Mix the cornflour with 30ml (2 tbsp) water and mix into the berry juice, stirring constantly.

○ Add the prepared berries and allow to simmer for 5 minutes on the lowest heat. Cool a little.

○ Put the fruit into a glass bowl, and sprinkle the surface with a little extra sugar (to prevent a skin forming). Allow to cool and place in the refrigerator.

○ To make the vanilla sauce, beat together the egg yolks and sugar until creamy. Heat the milk and vanilla pod in a pan, scrape the seeds out into the milk, and pour the milk into the egg yolks, beating all the time.

○ Pour the egg mixture back into the pan and, stirring all the time, heat until just below boiling point. Allow the sauce to cool, and remove the vanilla pod.

○ Serve spooned on to individual plates, with a spoonful of the vanilla sauce on top.

TERRINE OF ORANGES
WITH RASPBERRY SAUCE
Pavé d'oranges à la sauce framboise

To turn the terrine out of its dish once set, dip the base of the dish carefully
into hot water then place a plate over the top and invert.
You could use orange juice in this recipe instead of apple juice for a more
concentrated orange flavour.

15 PEOPLE

18	medium oranges
8	leaves of gelatine,
	soaked in cold water and squeezed dry
550ml (1 pt)	clear apple juice
1	bunch of fresh mint leaves
40ml (8 tsp)	Grenadine syrup
100ml (4 fl. oz)	water
15	tiny mint sprigs for garnish
	fresh raspberries for garnish

Raspberry sauce

450g (1 lb)	raspberries
60ml (4 tbsp)	icing sugar
15ml (1 tbsp)	lemon juice

○ Pare the rind from three washed oranges and cut into thin julienne strips. Reserve. Squeeze the juice from these oranges.

○ Cut away the peel and white pith from all the remaining oranges, and carefully remove the orange segments. Remove pips. Reserve the juice from the segmenting, add it to the other quantity, and strain it through a fine sieve.

○ Dissolve the gelatine in a little warm apple juice then add to the remaining apple juice.

○ Add 100ml (4 fl. oz) of the strained orange juice to the apple juice.

○ Chill a 1.5 litre (2½ pt) china or glass terrine dish and spoon about 6mm (¼ in) juice over the base. Chill until set, then overlap some mint leaves to cover the jelly entirely.

○ Place the terrine in a large bowl of ice. Spoon a little jellied apple juice over each side in turn and press mint leaves on to each side. Chill until firm between each application.

○ Arrange half the orange segments on top of the mint leaves and spoon half the remaining juice over. Chill until set.

○ Arrange the remaining half of the orange segments on top and spoon the remaining juice over. Chill until set.

○ Place the orange rind julienne in a saucepan with the Grenadine syrup and water and simmer gently until almost all the liquid has evaporated and the orange strips have turned pink. Leave to cool. Add a little extra water if they become too syrupy.

○ To make the sauce, purée the fresh raspberries then strain through a sieve. Stir in the sugar and lemon juice.

○ To serve, carefully turn the terrine out of the dish, and very carefully slice. Spoon a little of the raspberry sauce on to each plate and centre a slice of the terrine on top. Decorate with orange julienne, a sprig of mint, and a raspberry.

SUMMER PUDDING LYN HALL

This dish is named for the many-talented Principal of La Petite Cuisine School of Cooking. She helped with the photographs for this book, and in many other ways, and I am extremely grateful for her friendship and advice.

Summer Pudding can also be prepared in individual moulds – see the photograph facing page 193. If wished, sprinkle the edge of the plate with icing sugar, which is a simple and exciting way of enhancing the presentation. If the fruit is at its best in flavour there is no need for added sugar in this simple and good recipe.

4 PEOPLE

8	thin large slices of wholemeal bread, crusts removed, and cut into rectangles
5g ($\frac{1}{4}$ oz)	gelatine
100ml (4 fl. oz)	water
	juice of $\frac{1}{2}$ lemon
150g (5 oz)	ripe strawberries
150g (5 oz)	ripe raspberries
150g (5 oz)	ripe blackberries
100g (4 oz)	quark, mixed with sufficient skimmed milk to give a thick pouring consistency (see page 34)

Raspberry sauce

300g (11 oz)	raspberries
60ml (4 tbsp)	icing sugar
	juice of 1 small lemon

Decoration

4	pairs of cherries on the stalk
4	raspberries
16	blueberries or bilberries
4	sprigs of mint
15ml (1 tbsp)	icing sugar

○ Line a 900ml ($1\frac{1}{2}$ pt) mould with some of the rectangular slices of bread.

○ Dissolve the gelatine in the water over a gentle heat, then stir in the lemon juice.

○ Strain and divide the gelatine liquid between three small saucepans.

○ Add the strawberries, raspberries and blackberries separately to these three amounts of liquid and stew gently until just tender.

○ Place alternate layers of fruit and bread in the mould, finishing with a layer of bread.

○ Make a hole in the centre and pour in any remaining fruit juice.

○ Cover with a saucer and weight down with something heavy. Allow to set in the refrigerator for a few hours.

○ For the sauce, press the raspberries through a sieve, and mix with the remaining ingredients.

○ Unmould the pudding on to a serving plate and carefully pour the raspberry sauce over the top of the pudding to cover it completely.

○ Decorate with fruit and sprinkle with icing sugar.

○ Fill a small greaseproof-paper piping bag with the mixed quark and milk, and snip off the end.

○ Pipe a circle of sauce around the outside edge, then, using a skewer, draw it through the sauce to give a decorative finish.

SMALL FRUIT BASKETS
WITH RASPBERRY AND PEACH SAUCES

Tuiles aux amandes aux fruits de la saison

The fruits for these baskets can be varied according to season and, because
they are uncooked, they retain the maximum amount of Vitamin C.
  You could fill the baskets with exotic fruits instead of the above summer
fruits. Working to the same weight, use papaya, pineapple, kiwi fruit,
mango and lychees. Serve the raspberry sauce with some low-fat natural
yoghurt instead of the peach sauce.

4 PEOPLE

100g (4 oz)	icing sugar, sifted
100g (4 oz)	plain flour
3	large egg whites
	a pinch of salt
	finely grated rind of $1\frac{1}{2}$ oranges
25g (1 oz)	flaked almonds
550g ($1\frac{1}{4}$ lb)	mixed berries, ripe and at their best (such as raspberries, blackberries, bilberries, strawberries, red or white currants, wild strawberries, loganberries or dessert gooseberries)
15ml (1 tbsp)	icing sugar for garnish

Raspberry sauce

150g (5 oz)	raspberries
15ml (1 tbsp)	icing sugar
	juice of $\frac{1}{2}$ lemon

Peach sauce

250g (9 oz)	very ripe peaches, halved, stoned and chopped
1	vanilla pod, split
45ml (3 tbsp)	water
	juice of $\frac{1}{2}$ lemon
150g (5 oz)	low-fat natural yoghurt

○ Mix together the sugar, flour, egg whites and salt to give a thick batter. Strain the mixture if necessary.

○ Add the orange rind and almonds and allow the mixture to rest for 2 hours.

○ With your fingers, spread the mixture into four 18cm (7 in) circles on non-stick baking sheets. Do not aim for perfect circles; I much prefer a ragged wild look (see colour plates, pages 184–5).

○ Bake in a pre-heated oven at 180°C/350°F/Gas 4 for about 8 minutes until golden.

○ Remove from the trays immediately and place each circle on top of inverted cups or small basins so that they droop into a rough basket shape. Leave until cold and firm. Place immediately in an air-tight tin.

○ For the raspberry sauce, purée and strain the raspberries, then add the sugar and lemon juice. Bring to the boil, and leave to get cold.

○ For the peach sauce, cook the peaches with the vanilla pod, water and lemon juice for about 5–7 minutes until soft. Add the natural yoghurt and mix well. Purée and strain. Leave to get cold.

○ Sprinkle the icing sugar over the baskets, and arrange the fruit in the baskets.

○ Cover individual plates with peach sauce first, then add the basket with the fruits. Garnish with the raspberry sauce to your own design.

SNOW EGGS IN VANILLA SAUCE CHRISTIANE

Oeufs à la neige Christiane

This recipe is dedicated to Christiane Schröder who helped with many of the dessert recipes. Her immense talent brought to life many of my ideas.

4 PEOPLE

3	egg whites
15ml (1 tbsp)	caster sugar
	squeeze of lemon juice
30ml (2 tbsp)	warm toasted flaked almonds, to garnish

Vanilla sauce

300ml (½ pt)	skimmed milk
1	vanilla pod
3	egg yolks
30ml (2 tbsp)	sugar
150g (5 oz)	low-fat natural yoghurt

Caramel

50g (2 oz)	caster sugar
30ml (2 tbsp)	water

○ To make the snow eggs, whisk the egg whites until stiff. Continue whisking, adding a little sugar at a time. Whisk in the lemon juice, and continue whisking until stiff.

○ Heat the milk in a large shallow pan with the vanilla pod. Spoon or pipe twelve snow eggs into the milk. Simmer very gently for about 4 minutes. Drain carefully into a clean teatowel.

○ Whisk the egg yolks and sugar together. Pour the hot milk over.

○ Place the egg mixture in a double-boiler or basin over a pan of simmering water and cook until the mixture thickens sufficiently to coat the back of a wooden spoon. Cool slightly.

○ Stir in the yoghurt. Strain and keep warm.

○ For the caramel, dissolve the sugar in the water over gentle heat. Boil to a golden caramel, then drizzle decoratively on to a non-stick baking sheet to make twelve caramel garnishes.

○ To serve, pour the vanilla sauce into four individual soup plates. Arrange three snow eggs in each plate. Top with caramel and sprinkle with warm toasted almonds. Serve immediately.

Snow Eggs in Vanilla Sauce Christiane (see page 192)

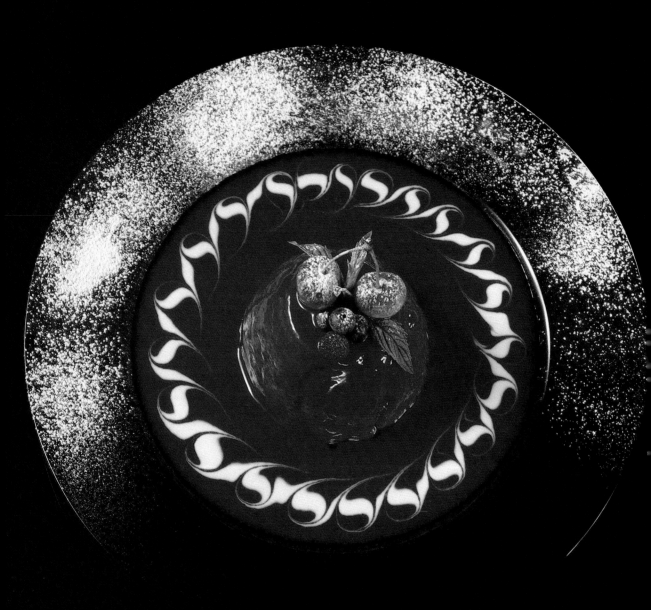

Summer Pudding Lyn Hall (see pages 188-9)

TIMBALE OF CHERRIES
WITH ORANGE SAUCE

Timbale de cerises à la sauce d'orange

4 PEOPLE

150g (5 oz)	black cherries, stoned
25g (1 oz)	caster sugar
150g (5 oz)	low-fat natural yoghurt
3	leaves of gelatine
200g (7 oz)	quark (see page 34)
8	fresh cherries, for decoration

Orange sauce

150ml (¼ pt)	fresh orange juice
25g (1 oz)	caster sugar
	pared rind of 1 orange, cut in thin julienne strips

○ Liquidize the cherries with the sugar.

○ Stir in the yoghurt until well mixed.

○ Soften the gelatine in a little cold water for a few minutes, then squeeze dry.

○ Dissolve the gelatine in 30ml (2 tbsp) water over a gentle heat and stir into the cherry mixture.

○ Whisk in the quark, then pour into four individual moulds and chill until set.

○ To make the sauce, place the orange juice, sugar and rind julienne in a saucepan. Heat gently until the sugar dissolves, then simmer until reduced to about 100ml (4 fl. oz). Cool.

○ Unmould the cherry timbales on to individual plates, spoon a little sauce around each one, and decorate with fresh cherries.

CARROT AND HONEY CAKE

Pain de carottes et miel

This cake, with the Vitamin A of the carrots, can be served at tea time as well
as for dessert.

4 PEOPLE

2	eggs, separated
50g (2 oz)	clear honey
	grated rind and juice of $\frac{1}{2}$ large *or*
	1 small lemon
100g (4 oz)	carrots, peeled and finely grated
100g (4 oz)	hazelnuts, very coarsely ground
	a generous pinch of ground cinnamon
	a pinch of ground cloves
25g (1 oz)	wholewheat grains, freshly milled
	into flour

○ Whisk together the egg yolks, honey, lemon rind and juice, until frothy.

○ Stir in the carrots, hazelnuts, spices and flour.

○ Whisk the egg whites until stiff, then fold into the carrot mixture.

○ Transfer to an oven-proof dish and bake in the oven at 180°C/350°F/Gas 4 for
20–25 minutes until risen and golden and firm to the touch.

WALNUT CHEESECAKE

This is the Cuisine Naturelle version of cheesecake, baked without the
conventional biscuit-crumb-and-butter base.

10 PEOPLE

675g (1$\frac{1}{2}$ lb)	curd cheese (see page 36)
75g (3 oz)	soft brown sugar
3	eggs, beaten
100g (4 oz)	shelled walnuts, chopped
30ml (2 tbsp)	plain flour
10	walnut halves, for garnish

○ Beat together the curd cheese, sugar, eggs, walnuts and flour until evenly mixed. Pour
into a 23cm (9 in) spring-release cake tin lined with non-stick paper.

○ Bake in the oven at 180°C/350°F/Gas 4 for about 40 minutes until set. Leave to cool
then remove from the tin.

○ Garnish with the walnuts.

DATE PETITS FOURS

Petits fours aux dattes

Dates contain fibre and some calcium, iron and niacin (one of the B vitamins).

MAKES 24

300g (11 oz)	fresh dates, stoned
100g (4 oz)	toasted hazelnuts, skinned
30ml (2 tbsp)	thick pear (or apple) juice

○ Finely chop the dates and hazelnuts.

○ Mix together with sufficient juice to bind them.

○ Shape into twenty-four small ovals, and place in petits fours cases.

RASPBERRY STRUDEL

Strudel de framboises

8 PEOPLE

225g (8 oz)	filo paste (see page 38)
50ml (2 fl. oz)	water
15ml (1 tbsp)	icing sugar

Filling

550g (1¼ lb)	fresh raspberries (or blackberries)
50g (2 oz)	caster sugar
100g (4 oz)	toasted hazelnuts, ground

○ Be sure that the pastry is very thin, and cut it into rectangular sheets of about 60 × 30cm (24 × 12 in).

○ Warm the water and icing sugar together.

○ Layer up the filo rectangles, brushing each sheet with the sweetened water.

○ Sprinkle the raspberries with the sugar.

○ Sprinkle the pastry with the ground hazelnuts and top with the raspberries.

○ Fold in the two long edges of the pastry, then, with the help of a cloth, roll up the strudel from a short edge.

○ Place seam-side down on a non-stick baking sheet. Bake in the oven at 200°C/400°F/ Gas 6 for about 25 minutes until golden.

○ Dust with a little extra icing sugar before serving, sliced on the diagonal.

ALMOND BISCUITS

Biscuits d'amandes

MAKES 40 BISCUITS

4	egg whites
100g (4 oz)	caster sugar
150g (5 oz)	ground almonds
40	blanched almond halves

○ Whisk the egg whites until stiff.

○ Whisk the sugar into the egg whites, a little at a time.

○ Fold in the ground almonds.

○ Place the mixture in a piping bag and pipe little whirls on to non-stick baking sheets. Top each one with an almond half.

○ Bake in the oven at 180°C/350°F/Gas 4 for about 20–25 minutes until golden. Cool on a wire rack.

SESAME PETITS FOURS

Petits fours au sésame

MAKES 24 PIECES

1	egg
40g (1½ oz)	caster sugar
75g (3 oz)	wholewheat flour
75g (3 oz)	sesame seeds
	grated rind of ½ lemon
	a little milk (if necessary)

○ Whisk together the egg and sugar until frothy.

○ Add the remaining ingredients and knead to a firm dough, adding a little milk if necessary.

○ Roll out the dough as thinly as possible on a lightly floured board and stamp out 6cm (2½ in) rounds.

○ Transfer to a non-stick baking tray and bake in the oven at 180°C/350°F/Gas 4 for about 15 minutes until golden.

○ Leave to cool for a few moments before transferring to a cooling rack. Leave to go completely cold.

OAT COCKTAIL WITH FRESH FRUITS

Cocktail vital

This can be served as an hors d'oeuvre, but here it makes a healthful dessert. Any kind or mixture of fruit can be used.

4 PEOPLE

60ml (4 tbsp)	rolled oats
100ml (4 fl. oz)	skimmed milk
150g (5 oz)	low-fat natural yoghurt
60ml (4 tbsp)	honey
30ml (2 tbsp)	lemon juice
2	apples, 1 red and 1 green, washed and cored
500g (1 lb. 2 oz)	berries (strawberries, raspberries, redcurrants, blackberries, bilberries, depending on the season)
60ml (4 tbsp)	hazelnuts, toasted, skinned and chopped
4	sprigs of fresh mint
4	raspberries for garnish

○ Soak the rolled oats for 15 minutes in the warm milk, then mix with the yoghurt, honey and lemon juice.

○ Grate the apples and add to the mixture.

○ Cut up the berries (if necessary), and add to the mixture.

○ Mix in the chopped nuts, and serve garnished with the mint and raspberries.

POACHED FIGS WITH MINT SABAYON

Figues pochées au sabayon de menthe

4 PEOPLE

50g (2 oz)	caster sugar
250ml (9 fl. oz)	water
4	sprigs of fresh mint, well washed
16	small fresh figs, carefully peeled
2	egg yolks
5ml (1 tsp)	freshly chopped mint
	fresh mint sprigs to garnish

○ Heat the sugar in a pan with a little extra water, and boil steadily until caramelized. Remove from the heat and very carefully add the measured water.

○ Add the four washed sprigs of mint and simmer gently, stirring occasionally, until the caramel dissolves.

○ Add the peeled figs to the pan and cook for 1–2 minutes until just soft. Remove from the heat.

○ Remove the figs from the pan and allow to cool.

○ Strain the caramel syrup into a clean pan and boil to reduce to 150ml ($\frac{1}{4}$ pt). Cool.

○ Beat together the egg yolks, whisk in the caramel syrup, then continue to whisk in a basin over a pan of simmering water until thick and frothy. Stir in the chopped mint.

○ Spoon the warm sabayon sauce on to four plates, arrange the figs on top, and garnish with mint leaves.

SEASONAL FRUIT TERRINE, JANET

Poésie de fruits en terrine, Janet

I could not have evolved the ideas of Cuisine Naturelle without the enthusiastic and generous help of Dr Janet Gale, to whom this recipe is dedicated. I cannot thank her enough.

15 PEOPLE

8	leaves of gelatine, soaked in cold water and squeezed dry
550ml (1 pt)	clear white grape juice
1	bunch of fresh peppermint
100g (4 oz)	mango flesh, sliced
150g (5 oz)	raspberries or strawberries, sliced
200g (7 oz)	papaya flesh, sliced
100g (4 oz)	bilberries or blueberries
100g (4 oz)	black or green grapes, halved and pips removed
	slices of extra fresh fruit and mint sprigs to decorate

Raspberry sauce

300g (11 oz)	raspberries, puréed and strained
30ml (2 tbsp)	icing sugar
	juice of 1 small lemon

○ Dissolve the gelatine in a little of the warmed grape juice. Add the remaining grape juice and leave to cool.

○ Surround a 1.5 litre (2½ pt) china or glass terrine dish with ice. Pour a little of the grape juice on the base. Allow to set, then arrange peppermint leaves over the jelly.

○ Turn the terrine on to its side, and coat that side with a little of the grape juice. Allow to set and arrange mint leaves over. Repeat on the other three sides.

○ Place the fruit in layers in the terrine, pouring a little of the juice over each layer of the fruit, and allowing it to set before continuing with the next layer.

○ Chill the terrine for 2–3 hours until set.

○ To make the raspberry sauce, mix the puréed raspberries with the sugar and lemon juice. Chill.

○ To serve, turn the terrine out carefully on to a dish (dip the terrine briefly into hot water to loosen), and slice. Serve decorated with fresh fruit, raspberry sauce and mint sprigs.

BREADS

Home-made bread has very special memories for me. I was brought up, literally, in a restaurant kitchen, and the most potent fragrance of my childhood was that of bread baking in the wood-fired ovens. Even today, the unmistakable smell of baking bread evokes clear and powerful images, and the wonderful taste it had is still in my mind. Not surprisingly, I have a very special love for good, freshly made, tasty bread.

Bread is one of the world's oldest foods, as well as one of the healthiest. White bread - now somewhat less popular than it used to be - nevertheless provides some protein and B vitamins as well as minerals (particularly calcium) and trace elements. Wholewheat bread contains all these (except calcium), and a slightly higher proportion of vitamins and iron, as well as fibre from the bran content of the wholewheat flour.

Wholewheat - literally the whole grain, outer layer and kernel - is undoubtedly better for health, and can be eaten as cereal in mueslis, and as flour in bread, rolls and cakes. Wholewheat, in whatever form, is digested slowly - as a result, one's appetite is satisfied promptly, and this feeling lasts for a long period of time. Wholewheat grains, known as wheat berries, are becoming more widely available and, for the greatest benefit, should be milled just before use (light and air, as with vegetables, affect the nutrients in the grains). Hand and electric mills are available for use in the home (or a good strong coffee grinder), but failing this, buy the best wholewheat flour little and often to ensure quality and freshness. And always, after sieving, use the bran left in the sieve.

Other grains and cereals are valuable nutritionally, and rye, millet, barley and corn can all be used in breadmaking. The corn breads in this chapter are light and tasty.

MINT AND POPPY SEED BREAD

This bread can be served with salads or main courses.

MAKES 1 SMALL COB LOAF, FOR 10 PEOPLE

300g (11 oz)	wholewheat grains, freshly milled into flour
2	pinches of salt
15ml (1 tbsp)	celery seeds
15ml (1 tbsp)	poppy seeds
15ml (1 tbsp)	freshly cut fresh mint
15g ($\frac{1}{2}$ oz)	fresh yeast
225ml (8 fl. oz)	tepid water
1	egg, beaten, to glaze

○ Mix together the flour, salt, celery and poppy seeds, and mint in a bowl.

○ Mix the yeast with one-quarter of the water and leave for 10 minutes or so until frothy.

○ Mix the yeast into the flour with the remaining water to give a soft dough.

○ Knead on a lightly floured surface for 10 minutes, then shape into a round.

○ Place on a non-stick baking tray, cover with a damp cloth and leave in a warm place until doubled in size – about 25–30 minutes.

○ Lightly brush with beaten egg and bake in the oven at 200°C/400°F/Gas 6 for about 30 minutes. To test if the bread is cooked, tap the base. It will sound hollow when cooked.

SAVOURY SESAME BISCUITS

Biscuits à sésame

These savoury biscuits can be served instead of bread, with salads and cheese.

MAKES 24 PIECES

450g (1 lb)	wholewheat grains, freshly milled into flour
50g (2 oz)	rye flakes
2	pinches of salt
2.5ml ($\frac{1}{2}$ tsp)	ground coriander
15g ($\frac{1}{2}$ oz)	fresh yeast
300ml ($\frac{1}{2}$ pt)	lukewarm water
75g (3 oz)	sesame seeds
1	egg, beaten

○ Mix together the flour, rye flakes, salt and ground coriander.

○ Mix yeast and water. Gradually work into the flour mixture to give a firm dough.

○ Sprinkle the work surface with half the sesame seeds and knead the dough on it until all the seeds are incorporated and the dough is firm and workable. Cover with a damp teatowel and leave to rise for 30 minutes.

○ Roll the dough out on a lightly floured surface to a rectangle 30 × 40cm (12 × 16 in). Lay on a non-stick baking tray.

○ With a sharp wet knife, mark the dough into twenty-four rectangles, 5 × 10cm (2 × 4 in). Prick the dough with a fork, brush with the beaten egg, and sprinkle with the remaining sesame seeds.

○ Bake in the oven at 200°C/400°F/Gas 6 for 15–20 minutes until crisp and golden. Break apart and serve warm.

CARROT AND COURGETTE MUFFINS

Serve warm for a savoury and healthy breakfast.

MAKES 24 MUFFINS

225g (8 oz)	wholewheat grains, finely milled into flour
75g (3 oz)	plain flour
5ml (1 tsp)	baking powder
5ml (1 tsp)	ground cinnamon
2.5ml ($\frac{1}{2}$ tsp)	ground allspice (Jamaican pepper)
2.5ml ($\frac{1}{2}$ tsp)	ground nutmeg
2.5ml ($\frac{1}{2}$ tsp)	salt
3	eggs
100ml (4 fl. oz)	clear honey
100ml (4 fl. oz)	skimmed milk
1	small orange, all peel and pith removed, segmented and chopped
$\frac{1}{4}$	vanilla pod, split and centre scraped out
100g (4 oz)	carrots, peeled and grated
150g (5 oz)	courgettes, washed and grated
50g (2 oz)	shelled walnuts, coarsely chopped

○ Sift the dry ingredients into a basin. Add the bran from the sieve.

○ Whisk together the eggs, honey and milk.

○ Combine all the ingredients together, including the black vanilla seeds. Beat well until evenly mixed, then divide between twenty-four non-stick muffin tins.

○ Bake at 200°C/400°F/Gas 6 for about 15 minutes until risen and golden.

FLOWERPOT BREAD WITH ONIONS

Pain en pot à fleurs aux oignons

Flowerpots make good baking moulds. Wash new clay flowerpots and allow to dry well. Heat the pots on a baking tray for 30 minutes at 220°C/425°F/Gas 7. They will give off a lot of smoke! Allow to cool.

MAKES 2 LOAVES, ENOUGH FOR 15 PEOPLE

450-500g (1–1 lb, 2 oz)	strong plain flour
2	pinches of sugar
2	pinches of salt
15g ($\frac{1}{2}$ oz)	fresh yeast
175ml (6 fl. oz)	lukewarm skimmed milk
125ml (4$\frac{1}{2}$ fl. oz)	lukewarm water
100g (4 oz)	onion, grated

○ Sieve 450g (1 lb) of the flour, the sugar and the salt into a bowl. (The remaining flour is for sprinkling and kneading.)

○ Mix the fresh yeast with a little lukewarm milk, then add the remaining liquids.

○ Work in half the measured flour, sprinkle with a little of the extra flour, then cover the bowl with a damp teatowel and leave in a warm place for 15 minutes to rise.

○ Work the remaining half quantity of flour into the risen dough until it comes away from the sides of the bowl.

○ On a lightly floured board knead the dough for 10–15 minutes until smooth and shiny.

○ Sprinkle a bowl with flour and place the dough in it. Cover with a damp cloth and leave to rise in a warm place for 1–1$\frac{1}{2}$ hours.

○ Meanwhile, sauté the onion lightly in a non-stick pan. Add the onion to the risen dough, and knead well.

○ Divide the dough into two even pieces. Knead each piece into a ball and place in a foil-lined clay flowerpot about 12–15cm (5–6 in) in diameter (see above).

○ Cover the flowerpots and leave to rise again for 30 minutes.

○ Bake in a pre-heated oven at 190°C/375°F/Gas 5 for about 40 minutes until well browned.

○ To test if the bread is cooked, remove from the pot and tap the base. It will sound hollow when cooked.

CORN BREAD

Pain de maïs

Cornmeal is also known as polenta or maize flour. As it is a soft flour, it is
usually mixed with another flour to give the best results.

10 PEOPLE

160g (5½ oz)	cornmeal
100g (4 oz)	wholemeal flour
10ml (2 tsp)	baking powder
	a pinch of salt
65g (2½ oz)	curd cheese
225ml (8 fl. oz)	skimmed milk
1	egg

○ Sift the cornmeal, flour, baking powder and salt into a mixing bowl.

○ Beat the curd cheese, milk and egg together, and stir into the flour mixture.

○ Turn the mixture into a 20cm (8 in) square cake tin, lined with non-stick paper, and bake in the oven at 200°C/400°F/Gas 6 for 20–25 minutes until risen and firm to the touch.

○ Cool slightly then cut into sixteen squares. Serve warm with honey.

PICNIC FRUIT BREAD

Pain pique-nique

This fruit loaf is delicious for breakfast or merely as a snack.

MAKES 1 LOAF, FOR 10 PEOPLE

350g (12 oz)	wholewheat grains, freshly milled into flour
	a pinch of salt
15g ($\frac{1}{2}$ oz)	fresh yeast
15g ($\frac{1}{2}$ oz)	fromage blanc (see page 33)
225ml (8 fl. oz)	tepid water
1	egg, beaten, to glaze

Filling

40g (1$\frac{1}{2}$ oz)	dried pears or apricots
75g (3 oz)	hazelnuts, toasted, skinned and coarsely chopped
40g (1$\frac{1}{2}$ oz)	cut mixed peel
50g (2 oz)	sultanas or raisins
	grated rind of $\frac{1}{2}$ lemon

○ Place the flour and salt in a bowl.

○ Mix the yeast, fromage blanc and about one-quarter of the water. Leave 5–10 minutes until frothy.

○ Add the yeast mixture and remaining water to the flour. Mix well to a smooth dough, then knead on a lightly floured surface for about 10 minutes.

○ Place in a basin, cover with a damp cloth or plastic film and leave in a warm place until doubled in size, about 40 minutes.

○ Meanwhile, prepare the filling. Soak the dried pears in hot water for 15 minutes. Drain and dry and cut into small pieces. Combine with the remaining filling ingredients.

○ Remove the dough from the bowl and knead well. Divide into one-third and two-thirds.

○ Knead all the filling ingredients into the two-thirds of dough and shape into a roll about 23cm (9 in) long.

○ On a lightly floured surface roll out the remaining dough to a rectangle large enough to encase the fruit roll.

- Place the fruit roll in the centre of the dough and wrap the dough around to enclose it completely.

- Place seam-side down in a 900g (2 lb) non-stick or foil-lined loaf tin.

- Cover with a damp cloth and leave in a warm place to prove until the dough completely fills the tin.

- Brush very carefully with beaten egg, then bake in the oven at 190°C/375°F/Gas 5 for 35–40 minutes until golden brown. To test if completely cooked, remove bread from tin and tap the base. It will sound hollow when cooked.

WHOLEWHEAT MUFFINS

Serve warm at breakfast or tea time.

MAKES 16 MUFFINS

300g (11 oz)	wholewheat grains, freshly milled into flour
10ml (2 tsp)	baking powder
	a pinch of salt
2	eggs
225ml (8 fl. oz)	skimmed milk
30ml (2 tbsp)	honey

- Sift flour, baking powder and salt into a basin. Add bran from sieve.

- Whisk together eggs, milk and warmed honey.

- Combine all the ingredients together and beat well until evenly mixed.

- Divide mixture between sixteen non-stick muffin tins and bake for about 15 minutes in a pre-heated oven at 200°C/400°F/Gas 6, until risen and golden.

CORN CAKE WITH PLUMS

Gâteau de maïs aux pruneaux

These plum squares are delicious for breakfast, or to accompany morning
coffee or afternoon tea. You could use apricots instead of the plums.

10 PEOPLE

150g (5 oz)	cornmeal
100g (4 oz)	wholemeal flour
7.5ml (1½ tsp)	baking powder
100g (4 oz)	clear honey
1	egg, beaten
	finely grated rind of 1 small lemon
60-75ml (4-5 tbsp)	skimmed milk, to mix
500g (1 lb, 2 oz)	fresh plums, washed
	icing sugar to garnish

○ Stir together the cornmeal, flour and baking powder in a bowl.

○ Add the honey, egg and lemon rind, then stir in sufficient milk to mix to a soft dough.

○ Press the dough gently into a 28 × 18cm (11 × 7 in) cake tin, lined with non-stick paper.

○ Halve and stone the plums and place, cut side down, on the dough.

○ Bake in the oven at 190°C/375°F/Gas 5 for 20–25 minutes.

○ Sprinkle with icing sugar, then serve warm, cut in squares.

Oat Cocktail with Fresh Fruits (see page 197)

Breads (see pages 201-8)

GLOSSARY

Al dente Usually applied to vegetables and pasta which are slightly undercooked so that they are crunchy or have some resilience to the bite.

Bain-marie A roasting or baking tray half-filled with hot water in which terrines, custards, etc., stand. The food is protected from fierce direct heat, and poaches in a gentle steamy atmosphere. It is also used for keeping foods warm and waiting, without the contents being spoiled by overheating or dryness. A double-boiler on top of the stove serves a similar purpose.

Bouquet garni Can be changed according to needs of recipe, but usually a mixture of parsley stalks, bay leaf, peppercorns and thyme wrapped with celeriac and carrots, and tied together.

A white bouquet garni consists only of onion, white of leek and celeriac plus herbs. It is used for white stocks.

Concasser To chop finely, or pound in a mortar. With tomatoes, skin, seed and chop into fine dice.

Coulis A liquid purée of fruit or vegetables, usually tomatoes, made without flour.

Court bouillon A seasoned liquid or stock in which to poach fish or shellfish.

Dress To pluck, draw (gut) and truss poultry and game.

Émincer To cut into small slices.

Escalope A thin slice of meat, usually veal, sometimes beaten out flat to make thinner and larger. This technique may be applied to poultry and some fish.

Fillet A prime cut of meat, fish or poultry, with all bones removed.

Fromage blanc *Fromage frais* ('fresh cheese') in France, for which there is no direct British equivalent, unless home-made (see page 33). Cottage cheese is too granular, curd cheese is too dry, and cream cheese has a more cloying texture. Fromage blanc has a light consistency, like thick drained yoghurt (from which a curd cheese can be made as well, see page 36).

Garnish An edible decoration added to savoury and sweet dishes to improve appearance, to awaken tastes, to add variety or colour.

Gelatine Leaf gelatine is used in a few recipes throughout the book, and should this be unavailable, use gelatine powder instead. One leaf weighs about 2g (just over $\frac{1}{8}$ oz), so use the equivalent weight of powder.

Glace de viande A good stock reduced to a glaze, for adding body and colour to sauces, prepared by reducing a basic beef, veal or lamb stock (see page 29). Poultry, game and fish stocks can be reduced to a glaze as well.

Glaze To cover - to improve appearance, by adding a gloss - with a thin layer of reduced meat, poultry or fish stock (for savoury dishes), milk or beaten egg (for pastries or bread), a reduction of stock or juices (for vegetables).

Hors d'oeuvre Usually simply means the first course, although the expression is sometimes used to describe a selection of savoury titbits served with drinks, or a mixed first course.

Julienne Meats, vegetables or citrus rind cut into long thin strands like matchsticks, not longer than the width of a soup spoon.

Mandoline A metal or wood frame with adjustable blades set in it for slicing vegetables finely, such as potatoes, cucumbers, etc.

Marinade A seasoned liquid in which to soak fish, meat or vegetables before further preparation to give flavour and tenderize.

Medallions Small rounds of meat, game, fish or shellfish, evenly cut. A *mignon* is similar.

Mirepoix The vegetable equivalent of a bouquet garni, often used as an aromatic bed for stews. It consists of roughly chopped vegetables (size according to need, and whether mirepoix is to be discarded or used as garnish), usually carrots, onions and celery, but turnips or other vegetables, plus herbs, can be added as well.

A white mirepoix for a white stock or sauce consists of onions, white of leek, celeriac, and added herbs.

Nutrients They are proteins, fats, carbohydrates, minerals, vitamins and water. These, even including a proportion of fat, are vital for good health. Fibre, although not strictly speaking a nutrient, is also necessary. All are available for the use of the body from fresh, well-prepared food.

Oven temperatures The following are roughly equivalent oven dial markings, not exact conversions.

Description	Degrees Celsius	Degrees Fahrenheit	Gas Mark
Very cool	110	225	$\frac{1}{4}$
	120	250	$\frac{1}{2}$
Cool	140	275	1
	150	300	2
Moderate	160	325	3
	180	350	4
Moderately hot	190	375	5
	200	400	6
Hot	220	425	7
	230	450	8
Very hot	240	475	9

en Papillote Literally, an envelope. A wrapping of paper or foil in which fish or meat is baked to contain aroma and flavour.

Petits fours Very small fancy cakes or biscuits served after a meal, usually with coffee.

Quenelles Most commonly, a light dumpling mixture of finely minced meat, fish, poultry or game - and egg whites - to be poached. A quenelle should be shaped like an egg between two warm tablespoons, and slid into simmering liquid to poach.

Suprême Choice pieces of poultry or game birds, usually the breast, and fish.

Terrine A china, earthenware, glass, metal or foil dish used for pâtés, potted meats, and some desserts. The word also applies to the foods baked or moulded in the terrine.

Timbale A thimble-shaped (but not -sized) mould for the preparation of savoury or sweet mixtures.

Tofu A curd 'cheese' made from soya-bean milk, known as *tofu* in Japan, but of Chinese origin. It has almost no taste of its own, but is rich in nutrients - the soya bean is the richest natural vegetable food known to man.

Yoghurt Yoghurt is formed from cow's, sheep's or goat's milk by the addition and action of benevolent bacillli. It is digested more rapidly and easily than raw milk, and its mild acidity is good for the stomach. It is a satisfying food, and is low in calories, especially when made with skimmed milk (see page 35).

INDEX